KENNETH BAKER

The Kings and Queens

*An Irreverent Cartoon History
of the British Monarchy*

WITH 204 ILLUSTRATIONS
58 IN COLOUR

THAMES AND HUDSON

To Amy and Marcus in their *Annus Mirabilis*

Half-title page:
Queen Victoria - probably the only sketch of a political
figure that Aubrey Beardsley drew.

Title-page:
Cummings's Queen Elizabeth II triumphantly leaps above
the problems created by her family in a cartoon specially
drawn for this book.

Contents page:
Cartooning came of age during the reign of George III,
depicted here in 1791 with Queen Charlotte.

British Library Cataloguing-in-Publication Data

A catalogue record for this book is available from the
British Library

ISBN 0-500-01705-0

Printed and bound in Slovenia

Contents

W ould Queen Victoria's heir make a suitable successor? Léandre gives the
French view of Edward VII in Le Rire, 2 February 1901

Preface

I would like to thank the many people who have helped me in the compilation of this book. First, Roy Douglas, of Surrey University, who once again has provided invaluable help in research, and also Rosemary Baker, for her historical guidance. Jane Newton, of the Centre for the Study of Cartoons and Caricature at the University of Kent at Canterbury, has been a mine of useful information and assistance.

May I also thank His Royal Highness, the Duke of Edinburgh for allowing me to include some cartoons from His collection; Lionel Lambourne for the use of two of his slides; the National Portrait Gallery of Scotland for providing a print of George IV; Michael Shea for three cartoons from his collection relating to the Crown and the press; John Ward-Roper for two of his cartoons from his private collection; the Piccadilly Gallery for permission to include two of its cartoons by Max Beerbohm; and the Executors or Estates of Max Beerbohm, Strube, David Low, Vicky, Illingworth, Osbert Lancaster and Giles. Lastly, I would like to thank the Imperial War Museum for the help they have given me, particularly in relation to the First World War.

My gratitude goes especially to the following contemporary cartoonists: Steve Bell, Peter Brookes, Bill Caldwell, Michael Cummings, Wally Fawkes (Trog), Franklin, Nicholas Garland, Griffin, Michael Heath, Hellman, Jensen, Kal, Leyden, Duncan MacPherson, McLachlan, Morris, Martin Rowson, Gerald Scarfe and Ralph Steadman. Finally, thanks to La Belle Aurore (Juliet Coombe and Steve Davey) for their skilled photography of many of the cartoons.

I have tried to find the owners of the copyright of all the cartoons that I have included, but some have proved elusive. I would welcome assistance in tracing them.

KENNETH BAKER
1996

THE KEYSTONE

Introduction

THE FIRST images of monarchs appeared on coins. Their profiles stamped onto metal were the evidence of their authority and the way that ordinary people came to recognize them as their leaders. The second stage of royal recognition was through heraldic symbols. The Prince of Wales in the 14th Century was identified by his plume of three ostrich feathers, and Richard III in the 15th by his heraldic beast, the boar. Apart from a handful of medieval paintings, the first royal portraits started to appear during the Renaissance and the first British monarch to be painted by an artist of genius was Henry VIII.

The portraits were propaganda, for few painters would either make money or, indeed, survive by being too frank. Holbein's great portraits of Henry VIII depict him as a large robust man, not obese, choleric and diseased; Van Dyck's romantic portraits of Charles I show him as elegant, noble and dignified, not short and petulant. The Winterhalter portraits of Victoria and Albert portray them as the ideal chocolate-box family. The patrons were usually the Kings and Queens themselves, who wanted their subjects to admire their strengths and not to be put off by their blemishes. Only Oliver Cromwell had the confidence and indifference to public opinion to insist that he should be portrayed with warts and all.

The first prints and engravings that were forerunners of the cartoon and that dared to question the authority and the status of the crown appeared during the struggle between Charles I and Parliament in the 1640s. Charles is attacked obliquely through his unpopular ministers, Strafford and Laud, though Cromwell is recognizably depicted in an unflattering way.

The most famous engraving of Charles I appeared after his execution in 1649 as a frontispiece to a book, the *Eikon Basilike*, which he was alleged to have written. It was republished again and again to give heart to the Royalists and sustain the prospect of a restoration of the monarchy. It is an early example of successful media propaganda.

As Queen Elizabeth II ascended the throne in 1952, Punch's Illingworth took the view that the monarchy was still 'The Keystone' in holding together a worldwide Empire.

So even at this early time cartooning was an extension of the political argument. It did not merely seek to represent the monarch. It carried with it a comment, either personal or political, and it took sides. Cartoons have to simplify the political message, for their success depends upon immediate visual impact. They are visual firecrackers that must make an impact within a few seconds, or else they will splutter and joylessly fizzle out. The best can be devastating and in a striking image sum up the weaknesses, the foibles, the deceits, the vanity and the silliness of their target. Unlike official portraits, they are not intended to be laudatory, their role is to be subversive, and they use one of the most powerful weapons against authority: ridicule.

Caricature, or *caricatura*, started in Italy in the late 17th Century. Annibale Carracci, its inventor, defined the caricaturist's task as: 'To grasp the perfect deformity and thus reveal the very essence of a personality.' Malice was there from the start, as was the intention to wound. This art form, in which England has excelled, took off in the 1730s with attacks on Sir Robert Walpole. Cartoonists need a big figure and few came bigger than Walpole. The King got sucked into the story because Walpole was attacked for the venal way in which he dispensed the patronage of the crown. George II became the first English King to be laughed at. One print shows him with his new mistress upon his knee and her hand upon his thigh; another shows him sending the British troops into battle while keeping back his favourite Hanoverian troops, and yet another his extraordinary habit of kicking anybody or anything when he lost his temper.

In the mid-18th Century, these prints were only seen by a handful of people who frequented the coffee houses in St James's, Westminster and the Strand. Hogarth made the art of engraving popular by producing prints that the affluent middle classes could afford to buy. Political prints really developed as an off-shoot of that. They were sold for sixpence each and hung up in the windows of the growing number of printshops in central London. Here they were seen by more people. Politicians and monarchs came to be recognized from their caricatures, at least as far as London was concerned, for very few ever reached the provinces.

George III, who ascended the throne in 1760, was turned into a fully fledged cartoon figure. At first he was shown as asleep, bossed by his mother, and blindfold as he led his country into the disaster of losing the American colonies. He was mocked, in a friendly way, for his great interest in farming efficiently his Windsor estates. He was also chided for his parsimony, for while extravagance has been condemned by cartoonists – George IV and Edward VII were also attacked for that – they do expect a King or a Queen to live in a regal way.

From the 1790s there was a distinct change in the way that George III was depicted. He had survived his first bout of madness in 1788 – there was only one cartoon which showed him in this state – and he had also seen Britain through the turbulence caused by the French Revolution. He became the symbol of the nation's resistance to the horrors unleashed by the Revolution and the champion to contain Napoleon's aggressive ambition. The country came to respect this straightforward, pious, basically decent man. Gillray, the caricaturist of genius, had no sympathy with the revolutionary excesses that were overwhelming France and he began to depict George III, who had been on the throne for thirty years, as one of the bastions of order and decency. When he drew the King as being made up of all the shire counties of England and defecating ships upon France, the people did not laugh at George III, but with him, for that is just what a good king ought to have been doing. George, who certainly saw many of these prints, never commented upon them adversely, apart from noticing in one that the details of the Windsor uniform, which he had designed specially for the Court when he was at Windsor, were not quite right. When he was approaching seventy, just before his final decline into senility, Gillray showed him as St George striking down Napoleon; his Golden Jubilee in 1810 was the first Royal Anniversary to be celebrated across the country and the Empire.

The engravings of George III during his reign reflect the changing nature of the monarchy. As the policy of the country, both in peace and in war, was determined by the politicians, the image of the King became more representational and symbolic. George III was conscious of his position as father of the nation and ensured that the royal portraits of him and his wife were sent to embassies around the world. He also developed significantly the ceremonial aspects of royalty. At his Coronation in 1760, he and his wife had been taken to Westminster Abbey simply and separately in two sedan chairs, but during his reign, parades, coaches, bands and soldiers in scarlet all became a more significant part of the royal presence.

George IV's reputation was certainly not enhanced by cartoons, some of which he tried to suppress, but which he could not resist collecting. But what a target – a philanderer from the age of sixteen, an inveterate roué befuddled by drink and drugs, with a string of

mistresses, an unstoppable spendthrift who could not resist collecting and building: at the same time a man of great taste and style who left behind him more fine buildings than any other English monarch. Compared with how he was treated by the whole galaxy of great cartoonists – Gillray, Rowlandson, Newton, Dent, Sayers and Cruikshank – the present Royal Family has been left relatively unscathed, though it may not feel it.

The 18th Century was an age of explicitness: members of the Royal Family are shown defecating, urinating, vomiting, farting and fornicating. There is no better way to capture the spirit of Georgian and Regency England than through these contemporary prints. And it was not just the King alone who provided the subject matter, for all his brothers were reprobates – the Duke of Clarence, later William IV, with his unofficial wife, Mrs Jordan; the Duke of York, the C-in-C of the Army, embroiled in the sleaze of selling commissions; and the Duke of Cumberland, who was almost certainly a murderer. All these were mocked and derided in the prints. They did not have the respect of the country, only its sullen and contemptuous allegiance.

If these prints had not appeared, then the images that posterity would have of George are the romantic miniatures of Richard Cosway and the flattering paintings of Joshua Reynolds. There is no doubt that he was hurt by the prints, for he tried to stop them appearing, either by bribing the engravers, or by sending his servants out to buy up the

*G*eorge III (far left) *actively participated in running the royal farms at Windsor. The words issuing from his mouth are in his usual staccato – 'Milk ho! Milk ho! Come my Pretty Maids, tumble out, tumble out, tumble out, above and below, above and below.'*

George IV (left), *as Prince Regent, built the most extravagant and exquisite little palace at Brighton, though his critics called it a royal folly. He was inspired by oriental architecture and the result was a gift for caricaturists: George's corpulence made him a natural mandarin.*

After the death of Albert in 1861, Queen Victoria (right) always wore black. William Nicholson captures her towards the end of her life – squat, formidable and unchanging.

copies and even the plates. Those he could not bribe, he tried to bully by threatening them with prosecution. But there were two snags. First, it is very difficult to prosecute a cartoonist for libel; and secondly, London juries refused to convict.

George was unlucky in that he was a victim of an advance in printing techniques. Woodcuts had been added to the song sheets that had been sold in the streets of London for many years, but in 1820 an enterprising publisher produced a pamphlet with woodcuts alongside the text. He produced a stream of satirical pamphlets in which George was depicted as a rouged, corseted dandy of sixty. These were published in tens of thousands and sold right across the country, which meant that the King's style of life became known to millions of his subjects.

William IV was the first King to benefit from the decline in the print trade and its replacement by national newspapers. Their readers, when they opened their newspapers in their drawing rooms, did not want the sniggering and the chuckling of the coffee houses. Victoria, too, benefited from this. Mr Punch cleaned up the cartoon and bent his knee to praise the Queen. She was such a contrast to all her uncles that in the public eye the monarchy was reborn. The only adverse publicity she received from cartoonists was when she became a recluse at Windsor following Albert's death in 1861. To have attacked Victoria in the press, particularly towards the end of her reign, would have been seen as an act of treason.

Clothes were a consuming interest for Edward VII (left). He loved dressing up and, when he travelled, was always accompanied by two valets, a footman and a brusher. He also became very fat. Breakfast lasted from nine to ten o'clock every morning, followed by lunch, tea and dinner, which regularly consisted of twelve courses. When he finished playing cards at one o'clock in the morning he polished off a dish of grilled oysters. It was no surprise that his ungainly form contrasted with the elegant slimness of Edward, Prince of Wales (right) in a cartoon now in the Royal Collection.

The more radical magazines had great fun at the expense of Edward, Prince of Wales, when he had to appear twice in court, once in a divorce action, and once over the Baccarat scandal at Tranby Croft. Although *Punch* was decorous, the other magazines had a good go at his lifestyle. The magazines on the Continent were much franker, depicting him as a womanizer and a heavy drinker, which he was not, and as a heavy gambler, which he was, and also as a cruel tyrant, suppressing the Boer farmers in South Africa. The British newspaper reader saw none of this. Edward VII benefited from what I would call the 'Accession Factor', namely, that when a Prince of Wales became King, the cartoons became more reverential. It even helped George IV in 1820 after the trial of Queen Caroline was behind him. The same thing happened to William IV, who on the whole was given a fairly easy ride, and it certainly helped Edward VII. The cartoonists became much more respectful, though to an extent that reflected the changes that took place. Edward VII was a poor Prince of Wales but a good King – just as Edward VIII was a good Prince of Wales and a very poor King.

In the 20th Century, cartoonists have in general been much more respectful towards the monarch. That has been due to a number of factors. First, the monarch has become a figurehead with no significant political or constitutional power. The power of the monarchy accords to Bagehot's famous dictum that it has 'The right to be

This cartoon by Kal, the Canadian cartoonist, contrasts the attitude of the Queen and of Margaret Thatcher towards the Commonwealth. At the biennial meeting of the Heads of Commonwealth nations, Margaret Thatcher was lectured on her policy towards South Africa, though it was vindicated by events. The Queen, who saw herself as a unifying force in the Commonwealth, was not so lectured.

consulted, the right to encourage and the right to warn.' The monarchy, therefore, does not share the odium of political failure. As Churchill said, 'In our island, by trial and error, and by perseverance across the centuries we have found a very good plan. Here it is. The Queen can do no wrong but advisers can be changed as often as the people like to use their right for that purpose.' Cartoonists, therefore, have concentrated much more upon the politicians. David Low, for example, one of the great 20th-Century cartoonists, only drew Edward VII when he himself was a young cartoonist in New Zealand, but did not include George V, Edward VIII, George VI, or the present Queen, in his later cartoons.

Secondly, both George V and George VI were Kings during two devastating World Wars; they became the representatives of the nation's determination to win. The soldiers who died did so for 'King and Country', and the memorializing of the dead became important ceremonies involving the monarch.

Thirdly, George V, George VI and Elizabeth II have all lived personally blameless lives. The fact that George V was dull was no disadvantage – he was happiest as the squire of Sandringham with a gun in his hand, or leafing through his stamp collection. It was disappointing, on the other hand, that he allowed the superb royal collection of political and satirical prints, which had been built up by his predecessors, to be sold to the Library of Congress in Washington D.C.

In Griffin's view, the wives of the present Queen's children threatened the stability of the whole monarchical edifice.

Queen Elizabeth's manner, style and behaviour have been the rock on which the monarchy has rested. Unfortunately, her children have not followed her example. Up until the late 1980s, cartoonists treated the Royal Family fairly gently: their interests were principally the horsiness of the family and the cost of maintaining the whole show on the road. When the Queen was criticized in 1957 by John Grigg, for her manner of speaking, he was physically attacked as he entered the BBC. Such champions of royalty have long since disappeared.

The marital troubles of Prince Charles, Prince Andrew and Princess Anne led to an onslaught by the media and cartoonists gleefully joined in. The satirical programme *Spitting Image* showed a family at war. In the 1960s and 1970s, the Royal Family had set about opening their lives and their palaces to the cameras and the press. It worked remarkably well until things started to go wrong. Then they found that their former friends in the press – cartoonists as well as writers – made the most of their troubles. Cartoons in the tabloids relished slap and tickle at the Palace. There were fewer cartoons in the broadsheets, but they were more trenchant. A politician expects no less, but a politician can answer back in the rough-and-tumble of debate. The Royal Family cannot, and when some have tried, they have just dug bigger holes for themselves.

The scurrility of the 18th Century returned. Cartoonists had such marvellous material, ranging from the arcane, erotic pleasure of toe-sucking and nude photographs, to offspring allegedly fathered in the

Antipodes. The sheer volume of the publicity, the relentless pursuit of the paparazzi, the gleeful exposure of every human weakness – all deeply wounded many members of the Royal Family and muddied the steps of the throne.

Has this done deep and lasting damage to the monarchy? Some have even argued that the monarchy cannot survive the unremitting glare of the tabloids. History provides perspective. It is not the first time that members of the Royal Family have been satirized for lechery, stupidity and selfishness. They were laughed at in the past as they are laughed at today; but laughter is a release: the derision and scorn have not turned into hatred. Republicanism in Britain today is as inert as it has ever been, for it has been suffocated by laughter. Everyone would have liked the marriage of the Prince and Princess of Wales to have been a happy one. But it wasn't – and the country with the highest divorce rate in Europe seems willing to accept that Princes and Princesses are mere mortals.

The fact that lampooning the behaviour of individual members of the Royal Family has not undermined the institution of the monarchy is due to the fact that during this period Queen Elizabeth II has been on the throne. She has fulfilled her royal duties with grace and dignity in spite of her family troubles, however hurtful they have been. The VE Day ceremonies showed her popularity and the affection in which she is held. The monarchy is safe in her hands – long may she reign!

While Queen Elizabeth II has been among the most popular of all British monarchs, would her eldest son survive the scrutiny of his private life, contrasted with his public role? Cartoon by Garland.

1 · *From Henry VIII to George I*

1509–1727

M OST of the political prints of the 16th and 17th Centuries were emblematic or symbolic. There were not many of them and most served as frontispieces to books of devotion. It would have been a brave artist in Tudor times who would have depicted Henry VIII or Elizabeth I in anything other than a reverential mode. The purpose of depicting monarchs was to enhance their status and to reinforce their authority. The enemy that faced the Protestant sovereigns of England – Catholic Mary Tudor and James II excepted – was the Pope and, from the earliest days, one of the truisms of caricature was established: the satirist must have a good, big target. Catholicism represented a threat to the security of the nation and so the prints depict the Pope as an evil figure, with a territorial, as well as spiritual, mission.

There was a sharp increase in the number of prints when Parliament, in the second quarter of the 17th Century, began to challenge the divine right of Charles I. The Great Rebellion of the 1640s, which led to the Civil Wars and the execution of the King in 1649, occasioned the first media war, for the prints were either pro-Royalist or pro-Parliamentarian. The King is rarely depicted and he is attacked through the Ministers whom he supported – the Earl of Strafford and Archbishop Laud.

The important drawing of Charles the Martyr in the *Eikon Basilike*, kneeling before the Bible and accepting the crown of martyrdom, was not in fact satirical at all. It was a romantic idealization of sovereignty and monarchy, and became a powerful piece of Royalist propaganda.

Caricaturists were not so kind to Cromwell. He is portrayed as a usurper who had made himself into a dictator, just as powerful as the Pope. The sharpest attacks came from Holland, where the art of engraving for political purposes was much more advanced than in Britain. In spite of the fact that Cromwell was a Protestant, the Dutch attacked him because he was a revolutionary figure and the leader of a country locked into a trade war with their own country.

THE PRESENTATION OF THE
BIBLE TO HENRY VIII, 1537

This is a woodcut that appeared in Foxe's Acts and Monuments, *first published in English in 1563. Henry VIII tramples upon Pope Clement VII, as he is handed the Bible in English by Archbishop Cranmer and Thomas Cromwell. The result is a good piece of* Tudor propaganda. The King's power, as demonstrated by the sword in his right hand, is absolute; the Protestant faith, of which he is the Defender, is triumphing over Rome. There is not a hint of satire and, if there had been, then that busiest of all the Tudor servants, the public executioner, would have been summoned.*

MARY TUDOR AND PHILIP II OF SPAIN, 1558

*N*o print of Mary Tudor survives, but this is a contemporary drawing of Philip and Mary which is placed in the initial letter of a Royal Letters Patent granting lands in Glamorganshire to one Thomas Stradlyng. The crown is shown above both Philip and Mary, although Philip spent only a few months in England. A child of this marriage would have ruled over England, Wales, Spain, the Netherlands and a very large part of both North and South America.

QUEEN ELIZABETH AS DIANA SEATED IN JUDGMENT UPON THE POPE, 1558

*E*lizabeth, as Diana, surrounded by her Protestant allies in Europe, watches Truth and Time subdue the Pope, as well as all the plots that the

Catholics are hatching. Although Elizabeth is naked, there is nothing lewd about the allegory. Goddesses were naked and no one would have assumed that this was in any way disrespectful. A Dutch engraving.

THE PROTESTANT QUEEN, 1569

*T*his stylized portrait appeared as the frontispiece of the Elizabethan Book of Common Prayer, *the printing in this version dating from 1569. Elizabeth is not only the Queen of England, but also the Supreme Guardian of the Protestant Faith. Patriotism and Protestantism stood together against Catholic Spain, which was busily engaged in preparing invasion from without and subversion from within.*

THE POWDER PLOT, 1605

*J*ames I receives a letter as he sits in one of the chambers of the Houses of Parliament. A devil, with a pair of bellows, blows on a torch by a conspirator (bottom left), *while an angel arrests Guy Fawkes (bottom right). This is not a satire but a piece of Protestant propaganda, which reminded the people of Catholic treason.*

ENGLANDS MIRACULOUS PRESERVATION EMBLEMATICALLY DESCRIBED . . ., 1646

Opposite

THE ROYALL OAKE OF BRITTAYNE, 1649

*T*he Ark of the Constitution is buffeted by the waves in which the Royalists are sinking. Archbishop Laud and the Earl of Strafford, both executed five years earlier, are in the water, as is Prince Rupert who is wielding a sword. On the left, Charles is kept afloat by hanging onto his wife, Henrietta Maria. Parliamentarian generals are bottom left (Fairfax) and right (Cromwell). By 1646, Charles had been defeated in the first Civil War and the long negotiations with Cromwell, on the terms on which he would continue on the throne, had started. London, throughout the war, had been true to the Parliamentarian cause and the Puritan presses had produced many anti-Royalist pamphlets. This print by John Lecester is in that tradition; it was 'printed for John Hancock and . . . to be sold at his shop at the entrance of Popes Head Alley'.

*T*his pro-Royalist print shows Cromwell standing on a 'slippery place', over the mouth of Hell, as he watches his soldiers cut down the Royal Oak, which represents Charles I and the Constitution. From the tree's branches hang 'the Royal likeness', the Bible, the Royal Arms, Magna C(h)arta, Statutes and Report(e)s – that is to say, the very laws of the realm. Those cutting down the branches are probably members of the Upper House while Members of the Commons – the 'unknowing mob' – pull at the rope. One of the mottoes may be translated, 'When the oak falls, anybody can collect wood.' Cromwell utters the words from the Book of Kings, I, 'Kill and take possession.' Clearly God, who aims a thunderbolt at Cromwell, does not approve of the killing of a King, particularly one who claimed that he ruled by Divine Right.

EIKON BASILIKE, 1649

*E*ikon Basilike, 'The Royal Image',
appeared just after Charles I's
execution and it was purportedly
written by him. In all probability, it
was the work of a clergyman, Gauden,
but his draft was corrected by the King,
for it contains his own views on
kingship and the events that led to his
downfall. Together with its
frontispiece, the book became the most
potent piece of Royalist propaganda. It
was so damaging to Cromwell's regime
that John Milton felt compelled to
attack it for idol worship.

The print was engraved by William
Marshall, but the King, who was an
accomplished draughtsman, may have
drawn his own image and pencilled in
the mottoes. The printer confirmed
that Marshall drew only the side with
the ship in it.

Charles is shown kneeling before a
Bible to emphasize that he was a

Protestant, but he rejects the golden,
worldly crown for the martyr's crown
of thorns, and the eventual prospect of
a heavenly crown. This print was of
considerable historical importance, for
it not only made the executed king a
martyr, but it held the prospect of the
restoration of the monarchy. Indeed,
before that occurred in 1660, there
were at least 35 separate editions.

OLIVIER CROMWELL, 1653

*T*he Dutch caricature appeared
shortly after Cromwell had
dismissed Parliament with the ringing
words, 'you shall now give place to
better men'. Stag horns come out of his
hat, on which a raven perches. He is
shown smoking a pipe and wearing
spectacles, as does the owl that sits on
his shoulder. Though this is merely
disrespectful, it is one of the first
examples of an ordinary portrait being
defaced.

THE HORRIBLE TAIL-MAN
APPLIED TO THE BRAGGADOCIO
STATE OF ENGLAND, 1658

*C*romwell receives three crowns
from Fairfax in another Dutch
print. The great tail of gold coins issues
from Cromwell's backside and various
people are trying to cut it off –
including, at the end of the tail, a
Royalist.

THE SCOTS HOLDING THEIR YOUNG KINGES NOSE TO Y GRINSTO

Come to the Grinstone Charles tis now to late
To Recolect, tis presbiterian fate

You Coninant pretenders must I bee
The subiect of your Tradgic Comedie.

Jockie

Stoope Charles

THE SCOTS HOLDING THEIR YOUNG KINGES NOSE TO YE GRINSTONE, 1651

In 1650, the Scots had recognized the young Prince Charles, son of Charles I, as King, but their price was his being subdued and controlled by the Presbyterians of the Kirk. He had swapped control by Rome for control by the Scottish Church – 'For Kirk must rule, this is the tenet of the Romish schoole'.

The print is pro-Parliamentarian and anti-Scottish, as Cromwell at that time was suppressing political opposition in Scotland, which had rallied to Charles. Cromwell decisively defeated the Royalist forces at the Battle of Worcester in 1651.

Humour barely enters at this stage. Where it does, it is usually triumphant and scornful, as in the print in which Charles II's nose is held to the grindstone by the Scottish Presbyterians. This was the price for their support for his claim to the throne.

The next sequence of events that stimulated the printmakers centred on James II's attempt to re-establish Roman Catholicism, and his overthrow by William of Orange. The most elaborate and venomous prints were again engraved in Holland, but there was a handful in England that introduced humour for the first time – an orange knocking off the crown of James II. The Dutch prints are elaborate and heavy, the English ones are lighter, foreshadowing the great period of graphic satire that was to flourish one hundred years later.

The Tudor monarchs were respected but, for the first time, the later Stuarts were mocked and laughed at. Then came a hiatus. There are no prints of significance from the later years of William and Mary, nor Anne, and merely a handful from the reign of George I.

CHARLES II, LOUIS XIV, AND THE STATES OF HOLLAND. PEACE OR WAR?, c. 1677

*C*harles II is the embodiment of the Kingdom of England and his royal horse carries the arms of the country. He is being offered money by Louis XIV to side with France against Holland. Not to be outdone, a Dutch sailor, seen under the belly of the horse, is also bringing more money. Charles did accept bribes from foreign powers, for it was a good way to evade Parliament's control of the financial purse-strings.

QUALIS VIR TALIS ORATIO, 1688

James II was determined to restore Catholicism as the national religion. Here, he vomits up reptiles wearing papal crowns, mitres and Jesuit caps – 'Such is the quality of the man, so is the quality of his speech'. The reptiles are crying out, 'No free Parliament', 'Expulsion of heretics' and 'Breach of Penal Laws'. Beside the bed, the Lord Chancellor, the Lord Mayor of London and the Aldermen hold their noses and turn away in disgust. Through the window the sun is rising as a Dutch fleet sets sail.

James's wife had just given birth to a son, James Francis Edward Stuart, who was to become the Old Pretender. The baby is shown on the left, far too large for one newly born; he carries a windmill, which alludes to the rumour that a miller was really his father. Not only the child's paternity, but even his maternity was disputed. The story was circulated that he had been smuggled into the Queen's chamber in a warming-pan. It was important for the Protestants who opposed James to claim that the child was illegitimate because a great many people, including those who disapproved of James's religion, had immense reverence for the monarchy as an institution.

THE ARRIVAL OF WILLIAM III AND THE FLIGHT OF JAMES II, HIS ARRIVAL IN IRELAND, 1688

William of Orange landed at Torbay in November 1688 and marched on London. Within a few days James had decided that the throne was lost; he threw the Royal Seal into the Thames and fled to Ireland. This Dutch print celebrates the arrival of William, who is welcomed by a distressed and manacled Britannia. It is a good example of Protestant propaganda which was also got out promptly – nothing succeeds like success.

ENGLAND'S MEMORIAL, 1688

An English print (above right), rather more wittily, commemorates the success of William of Orange. A large orange knocks off James II's crown. His Queen, Mary of Modena, holding the young prince, says they do not like the smell of oranges at all. Another orange knocks down Chief Justice Jeffreys, who was hated for his exceptional savagery in punishing those implicated in Monmouth's Rebellion of 1685 at the Bloody Assizes. The Catholics are in flight and the Jesuits in league with the Devil, but the Eye of Providence protects the Orange Tree and the Protestant Church.

A BRIDLE FOR THE FRENCH KING, 1706

Queen Anne (right), attended by a griffin, runs forward to place a bridle over Louis XIV, who tries to flee but is stopped by Holland. Louis XIV's ambition had been checked in the War of the Spanish Succession and by 1706 his armies had been defeated by those led by Marlborough at Blenheim and Ramillies. There are few prints of Queen Anne, but this shows how significant England's role was in the struggle for power in Europe.

THE UNFEIGNED RESPECT OF AN ENGLISH TORY, TO THE QUEEN OF GREAT BRITAIN, 1710

This broadside, depicting Queen Anne, appeared just after a change of ministry, about which it rhapsodized:

O may this late renowned, deed you've done:
Meet with success, may every Pious Son;
Of thy New Parliament, applaud thy glory;
And boast the being, an honest hearted Tory.

George succeeded to the throne when he was fifty-four years old. Like many of the Guelphs, he had bright blue bulging eyes – the same characteristic was to be seen in George III, William IV, Queen Victoria and Edward VII. George much preferred Hanover to England. He came over for his coronation and stayed until the first Jacobite Rebellion was put down in 1715. When he returned to Hanover in 1716 the first of many rows with his son focused on the question of whether there should be a Regent in his absence and what powers his son would have. On coming back to Britain in 1717, George almost imprisoned his son

LE COURONEMENT DU ROY GEORGE, 1714

No caricature exists of George I, but this allegory was published in Holland on 20 October 1714. George is being crowned by the genius of the people while his son, later to be George II, is told by Minerva that the King is a

model of wisdom and prudence. The British Lion is chasing away fraud and discord, which are also being battered by Hercules and Mercury. The clear message is that the Protestant King is a good thing and his prestige must be enhanced by this flattery.

over a row about the christening of his grandson. The Georges did not like their sons, and the sons did not like their fathers.

There was no Queen. George had divorced his wife, Sophia Dorothea, twenty-one years earlier after she had an affair with the handsome Count Königsmarck. The Count disappeared, possibly murdered on George's instructions. He imprisoned Dorothea in the Castle of Ahlden for thirty-two years, and she never saw him or her children again.

George had two mistresses. Melusina von der Schulenburg, who became the Duchess of Kendal, was very tall and thin, being dubbed 'The Maypole'. Sophia Charlotte Freiin von Kielmannsegg became the Countess of Darlington; she was enormously fat and known as 'The Elephant and Castle'.

Like many German princes, George liked opera and he also enjoyed playing cards and gambling. But he had no intellectual interests. One of his more famous remarks, made in a guttural accent, was, 'I hate all Boets and Bainters'. He hardly spoke English, preferring German or French, and, as very few English politicians spoke German, the business of Government was conducted in French or Latin and Cabinet papers were prepared in English and French. Because of his absence and inability to handle business in a different language, the King rarely attended Cabinet. He was also discouraged from doing so because it raised the question of whether the Prince of Wales should attend as well.

In 1720, Britain was racked by a financial scandal when – after wild speculation in the South Sea Company – the South Sea Bubble burst, by comparison with which all 20th-Century 'sleaze' pales into insignificance. George and his mistresses were implicated, but were extricated by a rising politician, Robert Walpole. Walpole had originally attached himself to the Court of George's son, but switched judiciously to the father when the opportunity arose. In 1721, Walpole was appointed First Lord of the Treasury and began a period of twenty-one years in power, which is the longest any Prime Minister has served.

The circumstances of George's death were ironic. His estranged wife died in 1726, but he left her unburied for over six months. It was while he was travelling to her funeral in 1727 that he had a stroke. It so happened that he died in the very same room in which he had been born sixty-seven years before.

A TRUE PICTURE OF THE FAMOUS SKREEN, 1721

The closest that one gets to seeing George I or his companions is this print, where the woman on the right is thought to be his mistress, the Duchess of Kendal. The South Sea Bubble had burst and the cashier of the company had fled to Antwerp – hence the map on the wall to the right. It was thought that he knew all the establishment figures who had been speculating and acting improperly, including Aislabie,

the Chancellor of the Exchequer, and other Ministers, who are hiding behind the screen. The screen is in fact meant to represent Walpole and the symbols on it refer to various incidents in his life. He was thus protecting the King and the royal entourage.

The cashier who had done a bunk was not pursued vigorously, since Walpole did not want evidence coming out that would involve the King and his mistress.

2 · George II

1727–1760

'George I was always reckoned Vile, but viler George II'
Walter Savage Landor

GEORGE II had married the very beautiful and able Caroline of Ansbach, and during his father's lifetime they had set up a rival Court in Leicester House. Unlike his father, George II enjoyed a happy marriage, and it was reported that he regularly visited the Queen's apartments at 9.00 p.m. He was punctilious in these, as in other matters, and would wait with his watch until the happy hour arrived. But he was not averse to occasional extramarital affairs during his wife's lifetime and she does not appear to have been much disturbed by them. Shortly before her death, Caroline asked George whether he would remarry. The King replied, 'Non, j'aurai des maîtresses', to which the dying Queen rejoined, 'Ah! mon dieu! cela n'empêche pas.'

Queen Caroline governed her husband by a combination of bullying and sensual gratification. Walpole realized her importance and used her as a channel to influence the King. In his coarse Norfolk way, he said that he 'took the right sow by the ear'. A popular contemporary jingle ran:

> *You may strut dapper George,*
> *But t'will all be in vain;*
> *We know 'tis Queen Caroline,*
> *Not you that reign.*

George II's initial instinct on being told of the death of his father was to appoint his old Treasurer, Spencer Compton, Earl of Wilmington, as First Lord of the Treasury. That lasted for less than 24 hours before Caroline persuaded him to reappoint Robert Walpole, whose critics were soon to call him 'Prime Minister'. She knew that he was the only man who could get an increased Civil List and the payment of George's debts through the House of Commons. Walpole knew that in order to receive he also had to give.

Walpole had a deep understanding of human nature. He was brilliant in discovering how he could satisfy the little foibles and weaknesses of human character. The King once told him to buy one hundred

SOME OF THE PRINCIPAL
INHABITANTS OF YE MOON, 1724

*R*oyalty, Episcopacy and the Law are
caricatured for only being
interested in money and high finance.
The judge's face is a hammer to smite
anyone who dares to attack the
merchants of the City of London. The
Bishop is propped up not by principles
or religious belief but a pump which he
manipulates in order to spew out gold
coins. The King's Orb is a bubble and
his chain is a string of bubbles. After
the South Sea Bubble had burst in 1720,
stories kept on coming out of the

fraudulent activity of the high and the
mighty. On the top of the King's
sceptre is a crescent moon, which
alludes to the lunacy of the whole
affair.

This is an anti-Court and anti-
Establishment print by William
Hogarth. His own father had been
bankrupted by the failure of certain
great men to support him. Hogarth
had to etch to feed the mouths of his
family, but this did not prevent him
from showing the whole rotten edifice
of Court corruption.

THE FESTIVAL OF THE
GOLDEN RUMP, 1737

George II is depicted as a satyr and is recognized by his raised left foot. George was subject to violent outbursts of temper in which he used to kick his hat around. The habit had already been wittily attacked in a pamphlet of the same year for which the printer was arrested. The Queen is on the right, about to administer an enema with a clyster pipe. This was a traditional remedy to calm the King and to give him something of his own medicine. Walpole, on the left, is shown as a magician manipulating the whole scene.

Walpole also was the subject of satirical attacks, but he decided to act only against the theatre, since he considered plays to be more subversive than pamphlets or prints. He had clearly been the model for McHeath in The Beggar's Opera in 1728. It was alleged that he had arranged for a play to be written called The Golden Rump, which was a scurrilous attack upon George I. When he read it to the King, George II flew into a rage and demanded that all theatres 'be cut up by their roots'. This allowed Walpole to rush a Bill through Parliament censoring plays. It left theatre managers virtually only able to put on Shakespeare. Walpole did not seek to extend this censorship to prints, though, from time to time, he had some of the printsellers arrested and held for a few days.

SOLOMON IN HIS GLORY, 1738

Queen Caroline died in December 1737. Two years earlier George, on a visit to Hanover, had seduced a young married woman, Sophia Walmoden – an event that he faithfully reported to his wife. After his wife's death, he lived openly with this mistress, whom he created Countess of Yarmouth in 1740. In this print, his mourning clothes are hung on the wall, his sceptre falls from his hands, and the table bears wine glasses and tell-tale German sausages.

lottery tickets to send to Madam Walmoden. They cost £1,000 and Walpole was happy to charge it not against the Privy Purse but against the Secret Service – thus everyone was pleased.

Walpole retained power through his manipulation of royal patronage. Jobs, sinecures, appointments were all sold or given to ensure favours were received by way of votes in the House of Commons or support in critical moments. The Government was dubbed 'The Robinocracy' and subject to a great deal of satirical attack, both in pamphlets and prints. Walpole was, however, one of the great statesmen of the 18th Century. He ensured the consolidation of the Protestant Hanoverian succession. His principles of government were to avoid war, to encourage trade, to cut taxes and, above all, to do as little as possible, to let sleeping dogs lie. George II was indeed fortunate to have such an outstanding politician in charge of the nation's affairs for the first fifteen years of his reign.

After Walpole, George II depended upon the Pelham brothers – Thomas, Duke of Newcastle, and Henry – to maintain the Walpole policy. But another eloquent voice was beginning to be heard – William Pitt, later to be Earl of Chatham. Whereas Walpole believed that war led to poverty and higher taxation, Chatham argued that it led to riches, prosperity and glory and, what is more, through his eloquence he lifted the hearts and spirit of the nation. The King feared Pitt, for he preferred armies to navies, particularly as they could be used to defend his Continental possessions in Hanover. Eventually, from 1757, he had to accept that Pitt's blue-water policies were necessary to contain the power of France and to defend British trade.

Father and son loathed each other – George II thought his son, Frederick, the Prince of Wales, was 'the greatest villain that was ever born'. Queen Caroline thought he was 'the greatest beast in the whole world and we heartily wish he was out of it', and she refused to see him on her deathbed. Frederick himself died of a chill in 1751, but his widow, the mother of George III, continued to be a focus for political discontents.

The other child of George II who attracted particular fame was William, Duke of Cumberland. The Duke played a large part in the campaign against the Jacobite insurgents in 1745–46, and pursued the

THE SCREEN, 1743

This anti-Court print shows the power of patronage that flowed from the Crown through the King. Studded on the Crown are various jobs which were in the gift of the Crown, ranging from the Prime Ministership to the Page of the Backstairs. George II is offering 'Cockades for boys at £300 a piece'. On the right Walpole, as a harlequin, is rejoicing in the fact that through his manipulation of this patronage he has survived a censure motion in the House of Commons.

THE C—T SHITTLE-COCK.

THE C—T SHITTLE-COCK, 1740

A remarkably modern-looking print, full of obscene puns. All the characters are clearly recognized and there is a liveliness not characteristic of many other mid-18th Century prints. The King and his mistress, the Countess of Yarmouth, are playing shuttlecock with Walpole and his daughter. The shuttle is in fact the

Duke of Argyll, who had just resigned from Walpole's Government, since a coalition intended to replace Walpole had broken up. The Countess of Yarmouth says to George II, 'Your cockee my love mounts rarely in Yarmouth'. This is explicitly lewd and shows that the two most powerful men in the kingdom both kept mistresses.

broken remains of the rebel army after the victory of Culloden with ruthless savagery. The English sang Handel's 'See, see the conquering hero comes!' in Cumberland's honour, and commemorated him in the name of the flower Sweet William; the Scots recall him as 'Butcher Cumberland', and preserve his name for a noxious weed known as Stinking Billy.

For most of his reign, there was little sign of public affection for George II. In 1745, when the Old Pretender's son, generally known as Bonnie Prince Charlie, landed in Scotland and made a serious attempt to secure the throne, there was a sudden surge of loyalty for George and his dynasty. It was during this period that the National Anthem appeared, in its original form, 'God Save Great George our King!'

George II was always suspected of preferring Hanover to Britain. He led his own troops into battle against the French at Dettingen in 1743 – the last time that a British monarch led an army into battle. But the future of Britain's progress did not lie on the Continent but in the promotion of trading interests across the rest of the world, something in which George II showed little interest. Thackeray, who wrote a biting satire on the four Georges a century later, said of him: 'Here was one who had neither dignity, learning, morals nor wit – he tainted a great society by bad example; who in youth, manhood, old age was gross, low and sensual.'

THE CONFECTIONER GENERAL SETTING FORTH THE H-N DESERT, 1743

George II was the last reigning monarch to command an army in battle. The British Army had triumphed at Dettingen, but the King had held back his 16,000 Hanoverian troops, who are seen here lying on the ground while the British cavalry in the background is charging against the French. This was particularly resented, since their wages were paid by the British taxpayer. The blue sash of the Order of the Garter lies around the King's feet, while he wears the yellow sash of Hanover. George sheathes his sword and says, 'Nolo prosequi', 'I do not wish to pursue.' He was called the Confectioner because he 'preserved' his Hanoverian men. Clearly, this was a vicious attack upon the King's preference for his German possessions.

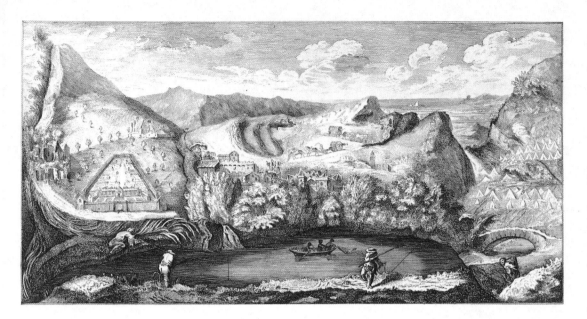

AN ACTUAL SURVEY OF THE ELECTORATE, OR FACE OF THE COUNTRY WHEREON HANOVER STANDS, 1743

The shape of George's face and hat represent the electorate of Hanover. George is wearing a large Kepenhüller hat. The print casts doubt over the value of Hanover to the British monarchy. The words at the foot read:

'Though this is not given as the most regular, the most varied, or the most noble prospect in the world, it is not doubted but it will pass for the most pleasant: and if it be free as Butler sings:
 "The real value of a thing
 Is as much money as 'twil bring",
Everybody must allow it to be the most valuable, because the most costly.'

The prints that featured George II emphasized his grossness, his sensuality and his love of Hanover. Although he reigned for thirty-three years, most prints come in an eight-year period, 1737–45, and there are none of any significance from the last fifteen years of his reign. The vein of satire was stimulated not so much by George II as by Walpole. The smaller number of prints that do survive from the last years of his reign feature Pitt and neither the King nor his heir appear in them.

On 26 October 1760, George II died in a privy at Kensington Palace. In theory, the Royal Prerogative had sustained little or no diminution during the reigns of the first two Georges; but in practice the authority and influence that George II transmitted to his grandson was very markedly less than that which Anne had enjoyed half a century earlier.

A VERY EXTRAORDINARY MOTION, 1744

The Government shuffle following the fall of Walpole is depicted in this print. The King, straddled across the table, evacuates Lord Hobart, the brother of his mistress, the Countess of Suffolk, but he is about to have to stomach another minister thrust upon him by the Prime Minister, the Duke of Newcastle, and his brother, Henry Pelham. The Minister whom they are thrusting down the King's throat is Sir John Hynde Cotton, who was a Tory with Stuart sympathies. The Pelhams were trying to create a 'broad-bottomed' government from all the Parties. Hynde Cotton was an exceptionally fat man, which adds a little to the irony. George is depicted in a supine position, thus with no real say in the formation of the Government.

No longer did the sovereign preside in person over the Cabinet and regularly play a major part in the day-to-day decisions of government. The first two Georges had more or less deliberately relinquished that power and it was difficult to see how a successor might resume it.

The sovereign could, and did, appoint the principal officials of Church and State; but his or her freedom to make such appointments had been much reduced. Ministers, usually though not invariably led by the First Lord of the Treasury, were coming more and more to 'advise' the King, and to expect that advice to be taken. First Walpole, then Henry Pelham and his brother, the Duke of Newcastle, came to preside over the vast edifice of crown patronage. It had suited George II that they should do so, for they were far abler than he was, and far more assiduous; and they also had good reason for preserving his throne.

Towards the end of George II's reign, matters took a further turn. William Pitt the Elder, later Earl of Chatham, acquired great influence – as the darling of the merchants of the City of London – although he was not *persona grata* to the King. Nonetheless, in the end, George was forced to take him as effective head of the ministry.

The first two Hanoverian Kings, whose claim to the throne was based on the Act of Settlement (1701), which disregarded fifty-eight better claims from Catholics, depended on a limited number of politicians and other leading citizens every bit as much as those people depended on the favours of the King. When at last a King succeeded to the throne who really did prefer Britain to Hanover, and who really wished to exercize the traditional powers of the monarchy, it was too late to re-establish the royal powers that had been lost.

THE WARMING PAN, 1745

*T*his is an anti-Catholic and anti-Scottish satire. Bonnie Prince Charlie is portrayed in women's dress, which he allegedly wore in his flight after the defeat of his army at Culloden. The picture in the warming pan is that of his father, the Old Pretender, and it alludes to a story that he was not the legitimate son of James II but had been smuggled into the Palace in a warming pan.

3 · George III

1760–1820

'George the Third
Ought never to have occurred.
One can only wonder
At so grotesque a blunder'

E.C. Bentley

WHEN George III ascended the throne in 1760, he was twenty-two years old, emotionally immature and politically inexperienced. He had learnt to read only by the age of eleven, and by twenty he still wrote like a child. As his father had died early, he had been brought up by his mother, whose Court – in true Hanoverian fashion – had become the centre for the malcontents. George therefore believed that the Government of the Elder Pitt and Newcastle, which his grandfather George II had accepted in 1756, was destroying the country, whereas it was in fact one of the most successful governments of the 18th Century. It had established British control over India and Canada, thus setting the foundations for the British Empire, which was to give Britain immense wealth, power and prestige for nearly two hundred years.

George, in his adolescence, had come to rely upon the personal and political judgment of the Earl of Bute. He was a surrogate father; when George asked him whether he should pursue his infatuation with the fifteen-year-old daughter of the Duke of Richmond and Bute said 'No', George dropped her. Instead he married the seventeen-year-old Princess Charlotte of Mecklenburg-Strelitz, who was dim, dull and ugly. She never mastered the English language and at her wedding she responded to the questions by saying, 'Ich will'. He remained faithful to her and produced fifteen legitimate children – a record for any British sovereign (even Victoria managed only nine). In the prints, Charlotte is depicted as a diminutive shrew.

Bute was not an important political figure before 1760, but George III made him his leading minister and First Lord of the Treasury. He was seen as an outsider, an interloper from Scotland, and the powerful factions that had roamed the political jungle since Walpole's days soon set about destroying him. They encouraged pamphleteers and print-makers to embellish the rumour that Bute was having an affair with

THE SCOTCH BROOMSTICK AND
THE FEMALE BESOM, 1762

From 1761 there was a spate of prints which implied that Bute and George III's mother, the Princess of Wales, were lovers. This is one of the most sexually explicit. The Princess of Wales says, 'Here's a besom for you', and boasts that she likes it more than Catherine the Great of Russia. Bute says, 'I am strong in hand.' One of the female onlookers comments: 'I wish my Sawney had such a broomstick.' There is little direct evidence of an affair.

George's mother, the Dowager Princess of Wales. The early prints of George III's reign focus upon this relationship and the young King hardly appears. Bute, who was lonely and in many ways as insecure as the King, could not stand this torrent of satirical abuse and after a little more than a year, he gave up office. But for years George III still turned to him for political advice – something that would be quite unconstitutional today. Queen Elizabeth II, for example, would not turn to Margaret Thatcher for advice upon John Major's appointments to his Cabinet.

The King was at sea without Bute. In 1766, in a typically immature *volte face*, he chose Pitt, whom previously he had loathed, as his close

YOU HAVE GOT HIM MA'AM IN THE RIGHT KEW, 1768

Even after George had been King for eight years, the Princess of Wales was still seen as the power behind the throne. Here, she leads her blindfolded son at Kew, where she lived close to the house of Lord Bute, to whom she is beckoning. James Townsend, a radical MP, said in the House of Commons in 1771: 'The Princess Dowager of Wales was the real cause of all the calamities which had befallen this country for the last ten unfortunate years.' This exaggerated her influence, but when she died in 1772 Horace Walpole recorded that, 'The mob huzzaed for joy.' Several prints from the 1760s show George either blindfolded or sleeping – clearly, not in charge of events.

FARMER G.....E STUDYING THE WIND AND WEATHER, 1771

George is again attacked for the neglect of state affairs. He prefers to spend his time in the royal nursery – the Prince of Wales is on the rocking horse – looking through the wrong end of a telescope at the fickleness of the wind and weather. His action is aped by a monkey; Bute, whose portrait is on the wall, rests his hand on the crown.

George was fascinated by astronomy. In 1768 he built an Observatory at Kew and in the following year stayed up to see the transit of Venus. He commissioned William Herschel, who discovered the planet Uranus in 1781, thereby extending the boundaries of the universe, to build a gigantic 40-foot telescope. His patronage of Herschel was in fact a major contribution to science.

THE HORSE AMERICA
THROWING HIS MASTER, 1779

*B*y this time, George III is clearly
seen to be in charge of events and
responsible for the humiliating defeats
in America. On each lash of the
scourge that he holds, there is a sword,
a sabre, a bayonet, a scalping knife or
an axe. The military force of Great
Britain had been broken by the
colonial rebels. George felt a personal
responsibility for the loss of the
American colonies, but the policies
that a succession of Ministers had
followed since the 1760s were really to
blame.

adviser. By this time, however, Pitt had become subject to fits of insanity. In his search for another father figure, the King found the Duke of Grafton, but he too was inadequate. Finally in 1770, he focused on Lord North, who was to be his First Lord of the Treasury and his Prime Minister for twelve years. It was to be an unhappy and disastrous coupling. North's weakness and slothful inadequacy gave him the unenviable title of Britain's worst Prime Minister. He presided over the humiliating loss of the American colonies.

The weakness of the men North chose to govern Britain put George III into a position that neither George I nor George II had experienced. He was identified closely as being personally responsible for the Government and responsible for its failings. The incompetence of North became the incompetence of George III. North's clumsy handling of the House of Commons was all George's fault and led to the belief that he was, like the Stuarts, seeking to increase royal power. All this was compounded by George III's own intense sense of duty – to preserve the rights of the Crown, the Protestant Church, the British Empire, and Parliamentary sovereignty by which the monarch and the

Houses of Parliament were jointly responsible for governing the country. His firm belief in these principles slipped into a dogged stubbornness.

George III should have learnt from Grenville's failure in 1765 to introduce a Stamp Tax on the American colonies that taxation without representation was bound to stoke the fires of resentment, which would in turn lead to rebellion. To defend the American colonies, Britain kept an army of 6,000 Redcoats, for which the colonists were obliged to pay

The rise of India stock & Sinking fund of Oppression.

THE RISE OF INDIA STOCK AND SINKING FUND OF OPPRESSION, 1784

The Fox/North Coalition of 1784 proposed to reform the East India Company. Many thought that their real motive was to get their hands upon the Company's considerable patronage. George III made it clear that any peer who voted for the Bill would lose his favour. In this print, the King is shown as the defender of the Constitution, as he cuts down Fox and North: 'To preserve Justice, Villainy must fall.'

The power of the crown was in evidence. Governments had to have the support of the King – after all, it was his Government. George then selected as his protégé the young William Pitt to be the new Prime Minister. No later monarch intervened so dramatically and so politically to bring down a government.

TEMPERANCE ENJOYING A FRUGAL MEAL, 1792

This is one of Gillray's finest cartoons. The King's modest tastes were seen as miserliness and frugality, and he was not liked for it. Kings were not expected just to eat eggs, and to drink oil and vinegar, and their consorts deserved more than a salad.

Every corner of the print reflects the meanness of the King – the patched breeches; the fireplace that has holly and mistletoe instead of wood; the empty cornucopias; the one candle that has burnt down; and an empty picture frame that bears the title, 'The Triumph of Benevolence'. There was no flamboyance at this Court, but austerity was despised almost as much as extravagance.

and to provide quarters. Britain also controlled their currency and their trade with the West Indies. If that was not enough, the colonial farmers were looked down upon, snubbed, patronized and denied any significant posts in the colonies where they lived. Rule from London was looked upon as a tyranny. Neither George III nor North had any understanding of this. George III looked upon the American demand for self-government as treason and the beginning of the end of the British Empire – if the American colonies were to be independent, then India, Canada and even Ireland would follow.

No monarch since the Stuarts had been so identified with a major national political issue and he suffered for it. After the defeat of the British Armies in 1781, George drafted a statement of abdication because he recognized that the failure was his. American children are taught that George III was responsible for all the many enormous mistakes made by his Ministers. One commentator has said that he experienced 'lucid periods of madness'.

In 1780, Dunning's motion that 'The power of the Crown had increased, is increasing, and ought to be diminished' was passed by the House of Commons. It spelt the end of North's administration, for he had lost the support of the squires and the gentry. There were calls for reform that were anathema to George III. Rockingham, who became the leading Minister, set about reducing the extent of royal patronage. The King was relieved when Rockingham died suddenly. Shelburne was the stopgap and after him came one of the most infamous couplings in the 18th Century, in which North came back to office and joined forces with the Ultra Radical, Charles James Fox. George III had to accept this extraordinary coalition under the nominal Prime Ministership of the Duke of Portland.

Portland introduced a constitutional novelty in that he refused to allow the King to discuss his choice of Ministers. The King could not stomach this, for the distribution of office, particularly the junior posts, was an important part of royal patronage. George III let it be known that any peer who voted for the Coalition's East India Bill would be regarded as an enemy. As a result, the Bill was dead; the Commons furious; and George ended this notorious Coalition by appointing as his chosen minister, William Pitt, the son of William Pitt the Elder. And that was the best political decision ever made by George III. Pitt loved power, was a moderate reformer, and above all an administrator of genius. He was to guide Britain through the aftermath of the French Revolution.

FILIAL PIETY, 1788

During George's madness he was kept at Windsor and virtually no one was allowed to see him, apart from the Queen. In November there was a rumour that he was dying; the Prince of Wales, frustrated by not being allowed to see his father, burst into his room.

This print, by Rowlandson, is the only one that depicts George III in his madness. It is also sharply critical of the Prince of Wales and his friends, Sheridan and Hanger, who are rejoicing at the prospect of the Prince becoming Regent, the sacking of Pitt, and the appointment of themselves and Fox as Ministers. Most of the prints at this time are favourable to the Prince of Wales, since it was likely that he would soon take over. Yet the King survived his treatment. When he suddenly recovered in February 1789, the Regency Crisis was over. Pitt remained as First Lord of the Treasury; and Fox was going to have to wait for seventeen years before he got office, and then only for a few months before he died.

In October 1788, the King succumbed to a first period of madness. It began with cramp, severe rheumatism and a rash. The whites of his eyes turned yellow, his speech was slurred, he became incoherent, he foamed at the mouth. He said to the Duke of York, 'I wish to God I may die for I am going to be mad.' He attacked his servants and told his barber to shave only one side of his face but not the other. He physically attacked his children.

Recently, medical experts have suggested that this illness was a virulent form of a rare hereditary metabolic disorder known as porphyria.

How pleasant is my dwelling place

London Pub by W. Holland, Oxford Street, May. 17. 1792

PSALM SINGING IN THE CHAPEL, 1792

George III started each day by attending a service at 8.00 a.m. in his private chapel which lasted for well over an hour. He had an unshakeable belief in God, and in his letters he frequently refers to his 'trust in Divine Providence'; he believed that his Coronation Oath was the most solemn undertaking he had ever made. The psalm that he, his wife, the Princess Royal and Princess Elizabeth are all singing is, 'How pleasant is my dwelling place'. On Sundays, the Queen would read a sermon in English or German to her daughters.

VICES OVERLOOK'D IN THE NEW PROCLAMATION, 1792

There was a Royal Proclamation in May, 'For the preventing of tumultuous meetings and seditious writings', which was directed principally against the revolutionary writings of Thomas Paine. The Prince of Wales, in his maiden speech to the House of Lords, warmly supported it. In this print, Gillray portrays, 'Vices which remain unprohibited by proclamation and dedicated as proper for imitation and in place of the more dangerous ones of thinking, speaking and writing now forbidden by authority'. Gillray invites the nation to observe, admire and imitate the example set by the Royal Family: George III's greed and meanness; the Prince of Wales's drunkenness as he is carried home from a brothel by two nightwatchmen; the Duke of York's reckless gambling; and the Duke of Clarence caressing his mistress, Mrs Jordan. Thus the Royal Family was seen as a disreputable lot whose actions presented a much greater threat to the throne than the writings of Thomas Paine. Wellington described the sons of George III as, 'The damnedest millstones around the neck of any government that can be imagined.'

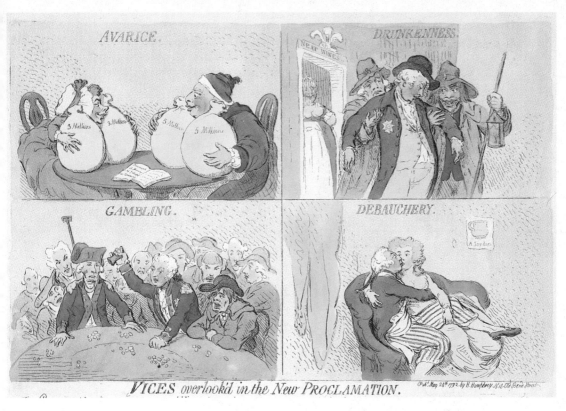

VICES overlook'd in the New PROCLAMATION.

It was known to affect members of the Stuart family and had been transmitted to the Hanoverians by the Electress Sophia, granddaughter of James I and mother of George I. The symptoms were the same as those from which George suffered and it led to hallucinations, apparent hysteria, paranoia and schizophrenia, and could loosely be termed madness.

George's treatment was primitive. He was given laudanum and various opiates, and was bled frequently. The doctors had no understanding of how to treat madness. Five or six different medical men were called in – the worst was Francis Willis, an elderly clergyman who had been granted a medical degree by Oxford University, and who allegedly had some skill in the treatment of madness. His technique was simple – he showed George III a straitjacket and said if he went on behaving madly he would be put in it. When George refused to eat or found it difficult to swallow, or became restless and threw off his bedclothes, Willis, his two sons and three keepers put him in the straitjacket. Later he was strapped into a chair, which he called 'The Coronation Chair', and was lectured by Dr Willis on his rambles. Willis stuffed a handkerchief into the King's mouth to keep him quiet until he had finished.

TAKING PHYSICK – OR – THE NEWS OF SHOOTING THE KING OF SWEDEN, 1792

Gustavus III of Sweden was assassinated in the Stockholm Opera House in 1792. Coming on top of the French Revolution, this shocked the crowned heads of Europe. Pitt is so worried that he even interrupts the King and Queen as they are jointly using the privy. This is one of the first glimpses of a bare monarchial bottom.

A BUGABOO, 1792

This superb print by Newton appeared just after Pitt had introduced severe measures to suppress seditious meetings and to stop the further dissemination of the ideas of Thomas Paine. George III, with Pitt on his back, shouts in his usual staccato way: 'Guard! Encampments!

Proclamation! Spies! . . . Informers! Confinement! Dungeons! Racks! Tortures! No leniency! No Mercy!'

Several societies and clubs were set up in London and other cities to spread Paine's ideas; in Manchester and Sheffield, troops had to be used to keep order. A 'bugaboo', however, is a bugbear that is an imaginary terror.

PRESENTATION OF THE
MAHOMETAN CREDENTIALS –
OR – THE FINAL RESOURCE OF
FRENCH ATHEISTS, 1793

*London was enthralled in 1792 by
the exotic Turkish Ambassador.
The political comment in this
engraving is very slight. It is the*
*dramatic obscenity of how the new
ambassador presents his credentials
that startles the King and makes the
Queen hide her face behind her fan. It
is also an oblique reference to Pitt's
lack of sexuality: he is portrayed as a
naked mannequin clutching the King's
knee in terror when faced by such clear
evidence of virility.*

During this illness the Prince of Wales and his crony, Fox, believed
that they were about to come into power. They started negotiations to
buy the *Morning Post* and Sheridan primed the *Morning Herald* with
anti-Pitt propaganda. Pitt had to introduce a Regency Bill, but he
ensured that it curtailed the powers of the Regent. As this was being
debated, however, the King recovered.

When the public got to know what had happened, there was a great
wave of sympathy for the King. It was soon suggested that the Prince
of Wales and the Duke of York had behaved disgracefully. They were
hissed and booed by the mobs in London as they went to the
Thanksgiving Service held at St Paul's in April.

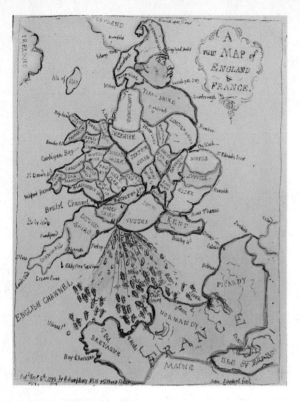

THE FRENCH INVASION – OR – JOHN BULL, BOMBARDING THE BUM-BOATS, 1793

*A*n amusing cartoon that was not meant to be disrespectful. George III, clearly representing the nation, uses the fullness of His Majesty to do just what his subjects want.

A PUZZLE OF PORTRAITS OR THE HOUR GLASS EXHAUSTED, 1794

*I*saac Cruikshank depicts the two profiles of Pitt and George III as an hour glass. The cartoon is a comment upon British defeats by the French. The Duke of York had to abandon Dunkirk in September 1793 and in December Toulon also had to be evacuated. The sands were running out.

Opposite, above
THE BRIDAL NIGHT, 1797

*G*eorge III was delighted to marry off one of his daughters, Charlotte, to the Duke of Württemberg. The Duke was immensely fat and Bonaparte said of him that 'God had created him merely to demonstrate how far the human skin could be stretched without bursting.' Gillray uses the opportunity to capture all of the royal princes. The Prince of Wales, in uniform, is fat and sulky; Prince William of Gloucester stands with splayed out feet.

The BRIDAL-NIGHT

TREASON, 1798

In 1798 there was a real danger that Ireland would help France by spreading sedition throughout England. Gillray, by this time sympathetic to Pitt and to the King, equates reform with sedition and treason in his prints. Newton, however, remained a radical and scornfully shows John Bull blowing a raspberry to the King, which Pitt declares to be treason.

This was one of the last cartoons that Newton published; he died the following year, at the age of 21.

This crisis had two consequences: firstly, the King became popular and the country came to respect its infirm monarch who struggled to be both good and noble; but secondly, the King was not able from that time to intervene closely in day-to-day politics. The real victor of the Regency Crisis was Prime Ministerial Government.

A further factor that added to George III's popularity was the French Revolution. When people read of the horrors of republicanism they were grateful that they had one of the oldest and most constitutional monarchies in Europe. The behaviour of George's sons was so coarse, vulgar and indulgent that this ageing, pious, dignified and basically decent man became popular by comparison.

THE KING OF BROBDINGNAG
AND GULLIVER, 1804

A brave attempt to depict Napoleon as a little figure, rowing about and amusing George III and Queen Charlotte.

ST GEORGE AND THE DRAGON, 1805

An important, patriotic representation of George III as St George. Although the King was old, and had experienced a period of insanity, Gillray depicts him as the national hero slaying the dragon Napoleon, who was at Boulogne while the combined French and Spanish fleets had put to sea. At the end of August, Napoleon marched his army away from the Channel coast to the Danube Valley, where he decided to fight and defeat the Austrians instead. In October, Nelson destroyed his fleet at Trafalgar – the crisis had passed.

George III's long and very eventful reign saw the King emerge as the epitome of the nation. He consciously enhanced the role of the monarch and he ensured that copies of his official portrait, by Ramsay, were sent to British Embassies and the outposts of the Empire. This representation of the monarch as a national symbol was an innovation that went out of fashion and was not revived until well into the reign of Victoria.

George III only intervened significantly in politics once again. This was in 1801, when he dismissed Pitt who, following the Union of Ireland and Great Britain, proposed to remove the various legal disabilities attached to Catholicism. George, in his simple old way, thought that Catholic emancipation was against his Coronation Oath and so he had to part with the Minister who had served him best.

Because of the threat of invasion by the French in 1803–4 George III – by now old, almost blind and seriously deaf – became the symbol of national unity. In 1811 he slipped finally into a long twilight period of insanity which was to last for another nine years. He was kept at Windsor where he wore a purple dressing gown, grew a long white beard and played to himself on a harpsichord. He had lost all touch with reality and spoke aloud of people and circumstances that had long since passed away. He was oblivious to all the dramatic events of the time – Napoleon's invasion of Spain, his march into Russia, his defeat at Waterloo and the economic and social depression after the war. By 1819, the governance of the country was in a critical state and Shelley penned his famous sonnet:

> An old, mad, blind, despised and dying king –
> Princes, the dregs of their dull race, who flow
> Through public scorn – mud from a muddy spring, –
> Rulers who neither see, nor feel, nor know,
> But leech-like to their fainting country cling,
> Till they drop, blind in blood, without a blow, –
> A people starved and stabbed in the untilled field, –
> An army, which liberticide and prey
> Makes as a two-edged sword to all who wield, –
> Golden and sanguine laws which tempt and slay;
> Religion Christless, Godless – a book sealed;
> A Senate – Time's worst statute unrepealed, –
> Are graves, from which a glorious Phantom may
> Burst, to illumine our tempestuous day.

GEORGE III'S GOLDEN JUBILEE, 1810

A kind and respectful drawing by Robert Dighton of George III on his Golden Jubilee. There was a great outburst of gratitude to the King on his Golden Jubilee and, for the first time, it became a subject of celebration throughout the Kingdom and the Empire. The country was saying 'thank you' to the King who had seen them through the loss of the American colonies, the threat of revolution, the establishment of a great Empire, and had also successfully resisted Napoleon's threat of invasion. In the City of London there was feasting and fireworks; Birmingham celebrated by erecting its first public statute; and, in over 600 towns in England, there were parades and parties.

GEORGE III IN HIS SENILITY, 1820

For the last nine years of his life, George lived as a recluse in a state of rambling senility in Windsor Castle. The Queen came to dislike even seeing him. Nevertheless, his death in 1820 was the first to be marked by national mourning and, at Windsor, a crowd of 30,000 turned out for what was meant to be a private ceremony.

4 · George IV

Prince Regent 1811–1820   King 1820–1830

'Whenever vice or lewdness lead the way,
With what officious zeal doth he obey!'

Anon., 'The Devil Divorced'

GEORGE had to wait until he was fifty-one to assume regal powers in 1811 as Regent. Up to that time, he had behaved much as other Hanoverians by becoming the centre of opposition to the King's Government – principally Pitt, later Addington and Perceval. At Carlton House, George gave succour to Charles James Fox, his drinking, gambling and whoring companion, who established single-handedly and for the first time the role of Leader of the Opposition.

George had observed from afar the mistakes made by his father, but he benefited little from this knowledge. He was aware of the powers of the monarchy and its significance as the head of the whole edifice of government. But his exercise of those powers was clumsy and somehow distant. In 1805 his father, in spite of his approaching senility, had been portrayed as the saviour of the nation. In 1815, after Waterloo, the Regent did not assume and was not given the same status. He lacked the power of single-minded concentration on political matters that George III had slowly and painstakingly acquired. He was easily diverted, giving more attention to the cut of a coat, the colour of a button, or the design of a chandelier, than to the dogged and often dreary business of governing.

A VOLUPTUARY UNDER THE HORRORS OF DIGESTION, 1792

This is a companion to Gillray's cartoon of George III (p.49). They were both etched in the same month, July 1792. Here is one of the great cartoons of the 18th Century. The Prince of Wales is shown as a man succumbing to indulgence. Once handsome and thin, his belly is now bursting; he is picking his teeth with a fork; apoplexy threatens. The chamberpot acts as a paperweight for the bills that have not been paid – at this time, tradesmen tried to stop the Prince in the street to claim their money. His medicines include cures for piles and a stinking breath. Two bottles are labelled Velnos Vegetable Syrup and Leake's Pills, which were quack remedies for venereal disease. The Prince had surrendered to the good life: it was quite usual for him to consume three bottles of claret at dinner.

WIFE & NO WIFE, OR A TRIP TO THE CONTINENT, 1786

*T*his engraving by Gillray is clearly a
fantasy, for George had 'married'
Mrs Fitzherbert in her house in Park
Street, Mayfair, on 5 December 1785,
and two of her relatives were the only
witnesses present. Here Edmund Burke
is shown as the clergyman whereas, in
fact, the person who conducted the
marriage was a penniless pastor
released from the Fleet prison who was
rewarded with £500 – marrying the
Prince of Wales without the consent of
his father was a felony. Fox is seen as
the best man, though he actually

opposed the marriage. Lord North
characteristically lies asleep in front of
the altar, seemingly unaware of the
wedding, but within days London
society was awash with rumours about
it. George and Mrs Fitzherbert are not
caricatured, which gives the greater
appearance of reality to the whole
scene. The Royal Marriages Act of
1772 had made any marriage by a
descendant of George II, under the age
of 25, unlawful and void without the
consent of the sovereign. The Act of
Settlement of 1701 had debarred
Catholics or anyone who married a
Catholic from the throne.

DIDO FORSAKEN, 1787

In a debate in the House of Commons Fox denied that the marriage of George and Mrs Fitzherbert had taken place: 'It was a miserable calumny and I am speaking with the authority of the Prince of Wales.' Mrs Fitzherbert's crown is blown off by Pitt; her breast is bare and the girdle of chastity broken at her waist. She sits on what appears to be a pile of money bags, which on closer inspection turn out to be a pile of penises. This is one of Gillray's clever double-entendres, for the House of Commons was soon asked to pay off the Prince's debts.

When George became Regent in 1811, the Whigs, then led by Grey, expected the Tory Prime Minister, Perceval, to be dismissed and for them to be given the fruits of office at last. By that time, however, George was not too keen on their policies, which had changed little since the old Fox days – peace with France, Catholic emancipation, the abolition of slavery and constitutional reform, which would reduce the power and patronage of the crown. George had no desire to reform himself away, but for old times' sake he suggested a coalition, a

THE ROYAL MINUET, OR
SAWBRIDGE'S DELIGHT, 1788

*In an imaginary scene, the Prince of
Wales spanks Mrs Sawbridge, who*
*was a noted beauty of the day. She may
be a surrogate for her husband, who
was an articulate advocate of
Parliamentary reform and is depicted
as playing the fiddle.*

proposal that was rejected. From that time, George was happy to leave the Government in the hands of Perceval and, after his assassination, Lord Liverpool. Behind them both was the most popular man in the country and its most successful soldier, the Duke of Wellington.

George showed no interest in the condition of his people – but then neither did George III before him nor Victoria after him. He was insensitive to the economic and social plight of the country from 1815 to 1820. He pressed ahead, against his Government's wishes, with his grandiose plans for Brighton. He had no awareness of the gravity of the constitutional, economic, social and political crisis of 1819–20, which could have engulfed the crown. His reaction was entirely personal and petulant, for he was concerned only with the scurrility of the attacks upon his person, wishing to stop them instead of addressing the behaviour which prompted them. By that time, he was far too set in his ways to change.

George's reign almost became the shortest in history, for he was too ill to visit his dying father and in January 1820 almost died within

THE LOVER'S DREAM, 1795

The Prince had agreed to marry, provided that his debts were paid and his income was increased. He dreams of his father holding out a large money bag of £150,000. His friends, Fox and Sheridan, flee in alarm, while his mistresses, Mrs Fitzherbert and Lady Jersey, are shocked. The Prince also dreams of a beautiful, slender Princess, but in reality when he first saw her he was so shocked by her coarseness that he immediately asked for a glass of brandy.

hours of his accession. On becoming King, George was content to leave the Government in the hands of Liverpool, who had been Prime Minister for the previous eight years. When Liverpool's health collapsed in 1827, George had to face his first real political crisis. Much to the chagrin of Wellington, he appointed Canning, then Foreign Secretary. Earlier in his life, George had disliked Canning intensely because of rumours that he had had an affair with Caroline. Most of the Tories deserted Canning, who died unexpectedly after one hundred days as Prime Minister. George appointed Goderich, but this stopgap lasted for only a few months.

OH! CHE BOCCONE!, 1795

*C*aroline and George were married on 8 April 1795 and probably only slept together for one or two nights – long enough for her to conceive a daughter who was born almost nine months to the day afterwards on 7 January 1796. Melbourne observed at the wedding that the Prince of Wales was 'quite drunk'. The cartoonist recognizes that George required some psychological assistance to perform his marital duties, for on the table beside him is a bottle of the aphrodisiac, Cartharides. They soon separated and Caroline lived a life of her own in London until 1813. The translation of the title of this print is: 'Oh! What a mouthful!'

FASHIONABLE JOCKEYSHIP, 1796

*L*ady Jersey, a matron of fifty, was George's mistress from the early 1790s. She encouraged him to marry in order to snub Mrs Fitzherbert: Wellington said, 'Lady Jersey made the marriage.' Here the Prince is wearing the uniform of the Light Regiment, of which he was the Colonel. He mounts the back of the Earl of Jersey, whom he had appointed as Master of the King's Horse four years earlier and who was clearly compliant with his wife's relationship. This print is one of the most savage and cruel comments upon the Prince's behaviour; it was the one that, more than anything else, turned the Prince against the press.

ENCHANTMENTS LATELY SEEN UPON THE MOUNTAINS OF WALES, 1796

There was a short reconciliation between the Prince and Princess of Wales, but it extended to nothing more than them dining together at Carlton House. The Prince of Wales is depicted as a goat – the symbol of sexual indulgence but the Princess is scarcely caricatured.

George then had to call for Wellington, who recognized that he would have to introduce a measure to allow Irish Catholic MPs to sit at Westminster, a consequence of Pitt's decision to create the Union with Ireland in 1801. This had been anathema to George III and George IV quoted his father's views to Ministers. On one occasion George IV begged Wellington for six hours – wheedling, threatening and weeping – to forego the measure. George then dismissed the Government; but this unusual exercise of the royal prerogative so exhausted the King that he virtually collapsed. Later the same day, he had to re-appoint Wellington. It was not possible to conduct the business of the country in this pantomime manner. George's conduct of affairs of state made it inevitable that in the future the powers of the monarchy would be further circumscribed.

George lacked the sinewy strength that all who wish to engage successfully in politics must have. He also lacked determined concentration; he bent with the wind; he was too malleable and he lacked a masculine tenacity. That experienced woman of the world, the Duchess of Devonshire, had hit upon this weakness back in 1782 when she observed, 'He is inclined to be too fat, he looks too much like a woman in a man's clothes.'

It is easy to condemn and deride George IV. After his death, *The Times*, in a priggish and ungenerous editorial, said: 'There never was an individual less regretted by his fellow creatures than this deceased King. What eye has wept for him? What heart has heaved one throb of unmercenary sorrow? . . . An inveterate voluptuary, especially if he had been an artificial person, is of all known beings the most selfish.'

Wellington, who had known George for nearly thirty years, was kinder, saying: 'He was the most accomplished man of his age. Upon every occasion he evinced a degree of knowledge and of talent, much beyond that which could be reasonably expected of an individual holding his high station.' He said later: 'He was indeed the most extraordinary compound of talent, wit, buffoonery, obstinacy, and good feeling – in short a medley of the most opposite qualities with a great preponderance of good – that I ever saw in any character in my life.'

THE RECONCILIATION, 1804

The relationship between father and son was appalling. The Prince of Wales once said, 'He hates me. He always did from seven years old.' George III despised his son's indulgence because he himself had to live very austerely to keep fifteen children. He had two effective measures of control over them. He could refuse them permission to travel abroad; and, following the Royal Marriages Act of 1772, he could deny them the right to marry whom they wished.

Pitt had pressed the King to have a formal reconciliation with the Prince of Wales and this was arranged at Kew in November 1804. The King is in Court dress, but the Prince's dress is tattered and dishevelled – his garter at his knee hanging loose. His mother is delighted to see it all happening.

When Hone, the radical publisher, was prosecuted in 1817 for producing a parody of the Catechism, he produced this print in Court, arguing that Gillray had used the Parable of the Prodigal Son. The defending counsel commented: 'Who was meant by either father or son, he would not say, but the gentlemen of the Jury might satisfy themselves.'

THE PRINCE OF WHALES, OR THE FISHERMAN AT ANCHOR, 1812

*T*he years 1811–12 were a watershed for the Regent. After June 1811 he saw nothing of Mrs Fitzherbert, who is portrayed in this print as the buxom mermaid holding the mirror, while the Prince looks at the even more buxom, but younger and more beautiful, Lady Hertford.

Politically, it was also a parting of the ways. The Liquor of Oblivion spurts out from one of the Prince's nostrils, falling upon his old friends, the Whigs – Grenville, Sheridan and Grey. They had hoped to get office and were now to be disappointed. Favour falls upon Perceval, standing in the boat, who has caught the great whale of the Prince Regent with an anchor which carries the words, 'Delicate Enquiry'. Perceval had supported the Princess of Wales in 1806 in the 'delicate enquiry' as to whether she had had an illegitimate child. He threatened to publish a written record, which would have been highly embarrassing to the Prince Regent.

This print also implies that Lady Hertford had considerable political influence over the Prince in determining his political preferences. It was inspired by a Charles Lamb poem which appeared some two months beforehand and was entitled 'The Triumph of the Whale':

Not a fatter fish than he
Flounders round the polar sea
See his blubbers – at his gills
What a world of drink he swills . . .
Is he Regent of the sea?
By his bulk and by his size,
By his oily qualities,
This (or else my eyesight fails),
This should be the Prince of Whales.

Yet George's very weaknesses were so undisguised, so open, so blatant and so human, that it is easy to forgive him a great deal. He was happiest when he was spending someone else's money on beautiful things. To devote a life to that was infinitely less damaging and harmful to the state of the nation than the activities of many other monarchs. As Prince Talleyrand said, 'Kings nowadays are always seeking popularity – a pointless pursuit. King George IV was "un roi grand seigneur". There are no others left.'

PATERNAL PROTECTION, 1813

*T*his very flattering drawing by
Robert Dighton portrays the
Regent protecting Princess Charlotte.
George was devoted to his daughter,
who certainly had a streak of
independence. In 1814 she refused to
marry the Prince of Orange, since she
would have had to leave England. She
was kept in close confinement near
Weymouth, where one of her maids
had to sleep in her room – she had
almost eloped with another man.

LEAP YEAR OR JOHN BULL'S PEACE ESTABLISHMENT, 1816

*T*he engagement of an obscure
German prince, Leopold of Saxe-
Coburg-Saalfeld, and Princess
Charlotte is celebrated. Leopold met
her at Brighton in February 1816, but
he was so hard-up that he had to take
premises over a grocer's shop in
Marylebone High Street. Parliament
was asked in March to provide him
with £60,000 a year and £10,000 for the
Princess. Poor old John Bull has to
carry this extra burden. The Prince
Regent is supported by two crutches of
gold and gives Leopold the advice by
which he had always lived, 'Push on,
preach economy, and when you have
got your money, follow my example.'
When the words, 'With all my worldly
goods I thee endow', were reached in
the wedding ceremony, Charlotte
laughed.

  She had two miscarriages and in her
third pregnancy, after a long labour of
50 hours, she had a large baby boy who
was stillborn. A few hours later she

went into convulsions and died
suddenly. The Prince of Wales was
desolate, but the Duke of Wellington
said: 'Her death was a blessing to the
country. She would have turned out
quite as her mother.' Leopold went on
to become King of the Belgians, having
turned down the Crown of Greece.

  The artist is Charles Williams, who
imitated Gillray. In 1819, he was paid
by the Prince Regent to suppress some
drawings.

ROYAL EMBARKATION, OR BEARING BRITTANNIA'S HOPE FROM A BATHING MACHINE TO THE ROYAL BARGE, 1819

*T*his cartoon was published just
three days after the Peterloo
Massacre had taken place and was an
explicit condemnation of the Prince's
way of life. Nine people had been
killed in the riot at the reform meeting
at St Peter's Fields, Manchester. The
Prince Regent decided not to return to
the capital, but to leave Brighton for a
visit to the Cowes Regatta.

ROYAL HOBBY'S, OR THE HERTFORDSHIRE COCK-HORSE!, 1819

*G*eorge Cruikshank could not resist using the new invention, the velocipede – the forerunner of the bicycle – to show how well it fitted the contour of the Prince, who is being ridden by the blowsy Lady Hertford. She wears a crown and the whip she wields is a sceptre. Her garter is inscribed with the motto of the Prince of Wales, 'Ich Dien', and floats from her ample thighs. George's brother, the Duke of York, rides another velocipede in the background. The pun is continued, for the Duke says his hobby is £10,000, which refers to the jobs and commissions that his mistress, Mrs Clarke, was selling.

NEW BATTLES FOR THE CHINESE TEMPLE, 1820

*I*n 1815 George asked the architect John Nash to apply to his Palace at Brighton the designs that the Daniell Brothers had depicted in India. Several times the Prime Minister, Liverpool, begged him not to spend so much on the Brighton Pavilion. George would not be stopped and within seven years he had spent £155,000, roughly equivalent to £10m today. At a time of acute economic distress, Liverpool urges the Prince Regent to 'consider the poor starving manufacturers'.

THE DANDY OF SIXTY, 1820

This is THE MAN – all shaven and shorn,
All cover'd with Orders – and all forlorn;
THE DANDY OF SIXTY,
who bows with a grace,
And has taste in wigs, collars, cuirasses, and lace;
Who, to tricksters and fools, leaves the State and its treasure,
And, when Britain's in tears, sails about at his pleasure,
Who spurn'd from his presence the Friends of his youth,
And now has not one who will tell him the truth . . .

*H*one, the radical publisher, produced a pamphlet with woodcut illustrations by George Cruikshank entitled The Political House That Jack Built, *which attacked the King and the establishment. Selling for a shilling, it went into scores of editions and rapidly became a bestseller. One of the King's friends considered offering Hone £500 to suppress it.*

AH! SURE SUCH A PAIR WAS NEVER SEEN SO JUSTLY FORM'D TO MEET BY NATURE, 1820

George IV decided that his wife, Caroline, should not be acknowledged as Queen. She had been living promiscuously in Italy and when she returned to England, he promptly sent evidence of her adultery to the House of Lords and the House of Commons in two green bags. For cartoonists these green bags became an endless source of fun. This cartoon by George Cruikshank anticipates by some thirty years the drawings of Philipon and Daumier, who turned people's faces into pears.

BERGAMI PEARS – OR – CHOICE FRUIT, 1820

Caroline appointed as her Chamberlain, Bartolommeo Bergami, who was a thirty-two-year-old Italian quartermaster; poorly educated, heavily built and swarthy. The British Government eventually agreed to send a Commission of three people to inquire about the Queen's conduct in Milan. One of the key witnesses was Giuseppe Sacchi, who had been a cavalry captain and had been her Equerry from November 1816 to November 1817 at Villa d'Este. He testified that he had seen Caroline and Bergami arm-in-arm and kissing many times. Occasionally, he had discovered them in the morning, 'both asleep and having their respective hands upon one another. Her Royal Highness had her hand upon a particular part of Mr Bergami and Bergami had his own upon that of Her Royal Highness . . . once Bergami had his breeches loosened and the Princess's hand was upon that part.' This is an explicitly sexual cartoon, which reflected the cries of the fruitsellers in London – 'Bergami pears and Caroline apples'.

THE QUEEN'S MATRIMONIAL LADDER, 1820

THE RADICAL LADDER, 1820

---

*T*he little toy ladder was drawn by George Cruikshank and sold with William Hone's pamphlet, which was published at the beginning of the Queen's trial in August 1820. In 1821, an indictment against it by the Constitution Association was thrown out by a Grand Jury.

The Radical Ladder *(above), which expressed the opposite view, was also drawn by Cruikshank, whose etching needle was for hire. It appeared in October 1820 and depicts the Queen climbing a flimsy double ladder, supported by little Jacobins, dangerous revolutionaries. She climbs up steps labelled Peterloo, Cato Street, Mob Government, Revolution, Anarchy and Ruin. This plate appeared as a frontispiece to the loyalists' magazine, a copy of which was presented to the King in February 1821.*

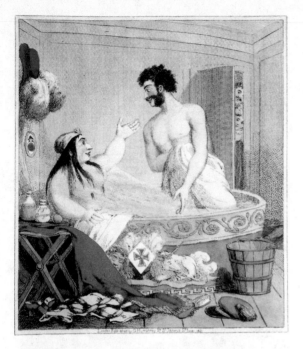

INSTALLATION OF A KNIGHT COMPANION OF THE BATH, 1820

O ne of the witnesses in the Milan Commission was Teodore Majocchi, who had entered the Princess's household in 1817. On a visit to Jerusalem, he reported, the Princess found it so hot that she had a tent fixed up for her on the deck of the ship, where she used to sleep with Bergami. He was also in her cabin when she was having a bath – Majocchi had to provide the water. She visited Jerusalem with him, entering on an ass, and established the Order of St Caroline of Jerusalem with Bergami as its Grand Master.

One of the squibs of the time was:

The Grand Master of St Caroline
Has found promotion's path.
He is made both Night Companion
And Commander of the Bath.

THE COMO-CAL HOBBY, 1821

T heodore Lane, a young actor with a gift for drawing, produced over fifty cartoons attacking the Queen in 1820–21. They depict her as a fat, sensual, vulgar, immodest person, with her lumbering, hairy lover. The title of this cartoon alludes to the lovers' rendezvous at the Villa d'Este, alongside Lake Como. Unfortunately Lane's surge of cartooning was cut short by his early death when, after a drinking session, he fell through a glass roof.

THE ROYAL EXTINGUISHER, OR
THE KING OF BROBDINGNAG &
THE LILLIPUTIANS, 1821

The King fought back. In January 1821 he turned the tables on Queen Caroline by publicly offering her a Parliamentary grant of £50,000 a year. In the previous November, the Queen had given a solemn pledge that she would refuse any offer of money, but from the moment she accepted the grant her popularity ebbed. On the King's left, the Prime Minister, Liverpool, and the Duke of Wellington, look on with delight.

George IV was motivated by one overwhelming passion – not duty nor honour nor dedication, but the pursuit of pleasure. He devoted his entire life to having a good time. He was truly the Prince of Pleasure. In that pursuit, everything was sacrificed – his family, his wife, scores of mistresses, the love of his people, the respect of his ministers, the loyalty of his political friends, his happiness, his health, and, in the end, his life itself.

George's splendid life was sustained by reckless extravagance. At the other end of The Mall from Buckingham House, which George III had bought for his large family because it provided some privacy, he built a magnificent palace, Carlton House, which became an alternative Court. Its rooms and ceilings were covered with gold leaf; the finest of fabrics were woven to cover chairs and curtains; furniture was specially designed; superb paintings were acquired; and elegant gardens

THE EFFUSIONS OF A TROUBLED BRAIN, 1821

*O*ne of the last cartoons in which Caroline is featured, for two weeks later she died. The popularity she had enjoyed in 1820 had evaporated and many regarded her attempt to gatecrash the Coronation in June 1821 as a consummate act of folly. Here it is suggested that she was partially insane, by that time living in a fantasy world.

were laid out. After George III's death, he turned Buckingham House into Buckingham Palace. As Carlton House was then too small, he pulled it down.

As Regent, he commissioned Nash to design the Royal Pavilion – the most extravagant little palace that any monarch of England has ever built. In 1824 he had over 800 workmen re-modelling Windsor Castle in the Gothic style under the direction of the architect, Wyatt. He also re-built the Royal Lodge at Windsor, his true home, where he laid out lakes and ornamental waters at Virginia Water.

George was particularly proud of the royal kitchens at Brighton, for he entertained lavishly. A dinner at the Pavilion, presided over by the great culinary craftsmen, Carême, consisted of a choice from 116 different dishes, served over nine courses with hocks, moselles, burgundies, clarets and brandies.

George had an abundance of good taste and imagination – qualities shared by very few of his predecessors or successors. He applied both these qualities to redesigning the centre of London. Nash was asked to design the beautiful houses now circling Regent's Park and to provide a road leading down Park Crescent through Regent Street and Piccadilly Circus, down the Haymarket and to Trafalgar Square, where the Royal Mews were demolished in order to build a National Gallery, the portico of which came from Carlton House. George left London infinitely more beautiful and elegant than he found it. No town planner has done better.

The Prince's private life was complicated. First, there was Mrs Fitzherbert, twice-widowed, beautiful and rich, who had come to live in London in 1784. She was also a Roman Catholic. She was fair-haired and had, above all, what the Prince of Wales liked: 'a fine bosom'.

Embarrassed by his overtures, she fled to the Continent, where she received love letters from the Prince, one of which was forty-two pages long. Before she went abroad, by an apparent attempt at suicide, he induced her to promise to marry him. They were 'married' secretly in December 1785.

In 1786 the Prince moved to Brighton, which was then a small fishing village, where he rented a house by the sea. Mrs Fitzherbert joined him and this was the closest that he ever came to domestic bliss. On his way to his marriage with Princess Caroline of Brunswick, ten years later, he turned to his brother, William, Duke of Clarence, and said: 'William, tell Mrs Fitzherbert she is the only woman I shall ever love.' Nonetheless, in his long relationship with Mrs Fitzherbert he had a number of other mistresses. In 1809 they finally separated. She was given an annuity, which was increased in 1830 to £10,000 a year, for she outlived him.

Before he died, George left instructions that he was to be buried in the clothes he wore during the night. When Wellington saw the King's body, he realized why he wanted this. Around George's neck there was a black ribbon and from it hung a diamond locket containing a miniature portrait of Mrs Fitzherbert. George took that with him to the grave.

George had the capacity to fall hopelessly in love. He was at heart a romantic, but few could match his stamina in succumbing time and time again. Sheridan acutely observed of his old friend: 'too much every lady's man to be the man of any lady.'

In 1779, at the age of 17, he fell for a very pretty Drury Lane actress, Mary Robinson, who was 21 years old. He sent profuse love letters to her, addressing her as 'Perdita' and signing them as 'Florizel'. She gave up her career on the stage and became his mistress. This affair lasted for only seven months, since his eyes had lighted upon the separated wife of a physician, Grace Dalrymple Elliott, by whom he may have had an illegitimate daughter.

George's letters to Perdita had to be bought back for £5,000 and an annuity of £500. George III, appalled by the 'shameful scrape' into which his son had got, even had to approach Lord North, the Prime Minister, for the money. Later Fox also had an affair with Perdita, but eventually he married a Mrs Elizabeth Armstead, who had herself had a brief affair with the Prince of Wales. Fox and the Prince were real cronies – bosom pals.

George had a succession of mistresses: Lady Jersey in the 1790s; Lady Hertford from 1807; and Lady Conyngham from 1820. They were all grandmothers, for he seemed to enjoy being dominated by mature women. By the time that George had become King, he was past any sort of physical intimacy. By 1826 he had also tired of Lady Conyngham, but recognized that, if the romantic spirit still flickered, the bloated body was not up to it. He said to Wellington, 'With my age and infirmities it is not worth looking out for another.' Caroline, when Princess of Wales, had put her finger upon her husband's behaviour: 'If he can but have his slippers under an old Dowager's table, and sit there scribbling notes, that's his whole delight.'

The foremost of the royal brood
Who broke his shell and cried for food
Turned out a cock of manners rare,
A fav'rite with the feathered fair. . .
But though his love was sought by all,
Game, dunghill, bantam, squab and tall,
Among the whole, not one in ten
Could please him like a tough old hen.

Caroline of Brunswick, who was a first cousin of George, was as surprised as anyone that the Prince of Wales had settled upon her to be the Queen of England. The Prince of Wales had wanted to marry for two quite laudable reasons – to clear his debts and to beget an heir. The choice he made was disastrous. George had not been told of her character, nor about the fact that she stank because she did not change her underwear. Like Henry VIII's Anne of Cleves, she had been wooed sight-unseen and it was too late to stop. They were married on 7 April 1795 and separated within days. A daughter was born nine months later.

Caroline remained in Britain, becoming very popular with the London crowds and the focus for resentment against the Prince of Wales. George in his turn resented the fact that she was cheered when she appeared at the opera. In 1806 a Commission was appointed to examine an allegation that she had given birth to a child in 1802. There was no specific proof but plenty of evidence of Caroline's immoral behaviour. Forbidden to attend official functions, she was refused a seat at the Thanksgiving Service in St Paul's to celebrate the end of the Napoleonic Wars.

The Prince and Princess of Wales established a practice, which was to be followed later, of using the press to further their own cases. The Princess was supported by the *Morning Chronicle, The Pilot* and *The Star*. Her friend, Lady Perceval, supplied the news in forged letters. In 1813, someone acting on behalf of the Prince of Wales tried to bribe the Proprietor of the *Evening Star* with £300 to turn against the Princess. None of this did the monarchy any good at all. In 1814, to George's great relief, Caroline – by then even fatter, dowdy and blowsy – left for the Continent, where she took up with an Italian adventurer, Bergami, who satisfied her voracious sexual appetite.

When George III died in 1820, the Cabinet decided that Caroline should not be Queen and was prepared to pay her an allowance of

OUTSIDE VIEW OF THE CROWN
TAP, 1820

This print by Marshall is not in the British Museum's collection and it may well be one that George IV tried to suppress. It shows him sitting in a boghouse as Little Jack Horner, pulling out a plum from the filth of the green bag. He is getting very blunt advice from a red-nosed Englishman.

£50,000 a year – roughly equivalent to £4 million today – as long as she remained out of the country. George IV insisted upon a divorce and the Cabinet reluctantly agreed.

Caroline's greatest supporter was the radical former Lord Mayor of London, Alderman Wood. He went to see Caroline and encouraged her to return. She followed Wood's advice and demanded transport from the Royal Navy for crossing the Channel. When none turned up, she took an ordinary packet boat. In the letters she wrote to Lord Liverpool, the Prime Minister, she signed herself as the Queen. The brilliant but eccentric Scottish Whig, Henry Brougham, had tried to dissuade her from returning, but when she was back in the country he used her in an attempt to bring down the Tories and get the Whigs in.

When Caroline reached London the diarist, Charles Greville, recorded: 'The road thronged with an immense multitude the whole way from Westminster Bridge to Greenwich. Carriages, carts and horsemen followed, preceded, and surrounded her coach the whole way. She was everywhere received with the greatest enthusiasm. Women waved pocket handkerchiefs and men shouted wherever she passed.' The windows at the house of Lady Hertford – George's current mistress – were broken and mobs shouted, 'Nero!' outside Carlton House. George IV sent a message to both Houses of Parliament recommending that they should examine the contents of a 'certain green bag'. This was a bag that contained the evidence of the Milan Commission, which had been burrowing away for four years to find evidence of Caroline's promiscuous behaviour. The delighted satirists focused upon the infamous bag.

After the Queen returned to London in June, Liverpool, the Prime Minister, brought before the House of Lords a Bill of Pains and Penalties which accused the Queen of having had an adulterous intercourse with Bergami; it would have deprived her of the 'titles, prerogatives, rights, privilege and pretensions of Queen Consort of this Realm', and dissolved 'the marriage between His Majesty and the said Queen'. It was an unprecedented Parliamentary procedure.

On 17 August 1820, a public inquiry began in the House of Lords. Brougham made some brilliant speeches and subjected the witnesses to devastating cross-examination. Half of these had refused to come from Italy because they believed they would be arrested and executed. Adultery with the Queen Consort, or with the wife of the heir-presumptive, was a capital offence, at least where the adulterer is a British subject. Brougham reduced Majocchi, who had been an equerry to Princess Caroline and a key witness for the Prince, to a gibbering wreck. Majocchi got so flustered that he kept on saying, 'Non mi ricordo' – 'I do not remember.' This became a catchphrase that was picked up by the satirists.

The Duke of Wellington, who was for the King, found himself surrounded outside Apsley House by some roadmenders who demanded that he had to say 'God save the Queen'. He replied, 'Well gentlemen, since you will have it, God save the Queen, and may all your wives be like her.' The crowds in the streets of London shouted, 'The Queen forever, the King in the river' and Caroline announced that her intention was to 'blow him off the throne'. The Queen's enemies produced a squib:

> Most gracious Queen, we thee implore
> To go away and sin no more;
> Or if that effort be too great,
> To go away at any rate.

On 6 November 1820, the House of Lords voted 123 to 95 against the Queen – a majority of 28. On the Third Reading on 10 November, the Whig success in marshalling national sympathy for her led to the majority falling to 9. It became clear that the Government would not get this Bill through the Commons and it had to be dropped. That was the high point of Caroline's campaign.

Brougham was determined to prove that George's green bag of infidelities was much larger than Caroline's. He had seen evidence of a will drafted by George IV in which he referred to Mrs Fitzherbert as his 'dear wife'. He was quite prepared to use that if the Bill proceeded. He had also found witnesses who were prepared to swear to the King's sexual escapades with the daughters of a turnpike man named Highfield, with a French courtesan, Madame de Mayer, and with Mrs Crowe, whom he kept in a house in Charles II Street just off St James's Square and by whom he had a child. There was also a Weymouth boarding-house keeper, Mrs Mary Lewis, and even a common prostitute.

The King and Cabinet decided they had to strike back and made public the offer of cash to Caroline, as well as the fact that she was inclined to accept it. The tide began to turn. Cartoonists were bribed to produce flattering cartoons of the King's address to the new Parliament in January 1821. A gifted young artist, Theodore Lane, produced a series of lewd and satirical drawings of Caroline and Bergami. When she attempted to enter Westminster Abbey for the Coronation, Caroline was politely told that she could not, for she did not have an official ticket. The London crowds no longer took up her case. Just a month later she suddenly died. Max Beerbohm wrote later that Caroline had been cast for a tragic role, but she played it in tights.

George himself was on a visit to Ireland. The news was given to him that Napoleon had died: 'Your Majesty, your greatest enemy is dead.' George replied: 'Is she, thank God.'

George's mistresses were only one relatively minor contribution to his recklessly extravagant lifestyle. In 1786 his debts amounted to £269,878.6s.7d – equivalent today to perhaps £20 million – but Parliament agreed to meet them and to fund his alternative Court at Carlton House. Just imagine Parliament's reaction if it were faced with that problem today!

George carried on spending and in 1809 his debts were over £500,000 – something like £40 million today. He knew that one day he would be King and the nation would pay – meantime, he was determined to enjoy himself.

George loved dressing up. In 1783, when he took his seat in the House of Lords, he wore a black velvet suit lined with pink satin, embroidered in gold, shoes with pink heels, and his hair frizzed and curled. A fortune was spent on waistcoats and cravats. He had pined for years to be a Field Marshal, for he liked parades, soldiers marching, bands playing and fully decked carriages. He showed a true sense of

THE FIRST LAIRD IN AW SCOTIA –
OR A VIEW AT EDINBURGH IN
AUGUST, 1822

George IV invented royal tours. He was the first King of England to visit Scotland with no intention of conquering it. As Crabbe, the poet, wrote:

Of old when a monarch of England
  appear'd
In Scotland, he came as a foe;
There was war in the land, and
  around it were heard,
Lamentation, and mourning and
  woe.

George relished appearing in full Highland costume, a rigout which cost him in current money approximately £60,000. He was welcomed by cheering crowds and Walter Scott, on this visit the official pageant master, recorded that the people's 'delight was extreme at seeing a portly, handsome man, looking and moving every inch a King'. The Scottish ladies were more interested in seeing what he wore under his kilt.

theatre and always wanted to put on a good show, which he did with great panache. He invented royal tours. Previously monarchs had only visited Ireland, Scotland or Wales in order to conquer them; George visited them to meet his people, who loved it.

A KING-FISHER, 1826

George arranged picnics at Virginia Water, usually accompanied by Lady Conyngham. On one occasion, he invited the seven-year-old Princess Victoria. This print shows the rebuilt Windsor Castle and the refurbished Royal Lodge, which William IV was to pull down. George IV was so angry at being shown catching a frog with the sceptre that he decided to stop fishing.

George craved companionship. He liked to cuddle and hold hands with Lady Conyngham, while her husband was happy to look on.

> 'Tis pleasant as the seasons to see
>   how they sit,
> First cracking their nuts, and then
>   cracking their wit:
> Then quoffing their claret – then
>   mingling their lips
> Or tickling the fat about each other's
>   hips.

THE CAMELOPARD, OR A NEW HOBBY, 1827

The Pasha of Egypt gave a giraffe (camelopard) and two attendants to George IV. The giraffe was kept at Windsor. The King's companion is the large-bottomed Lady Conyngham. The King added the giraffe to the menagerie of strange beasts that he kept at Windsor and he came to love it. It featured in many prints, but only survived for two years. George then had it stuffed.

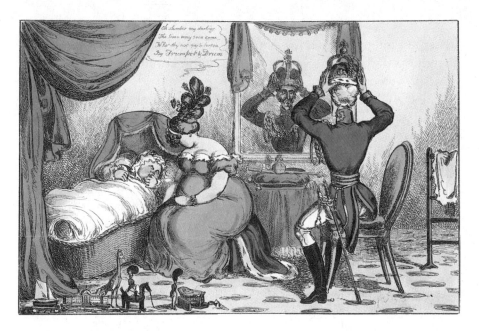

A POLITICAL REFLECTION, 1828

Following the collapse of the Government of the insignificant Goderich – a Prime Minister remembered for his capacity to burst into tears – Wellington had become Prime Minister and in this cartoon rests the crown on his head. Although Wellington was the obvious choice, Lady Conyngham was said to have had a hand in this decision. In the following year Wellington, reluctantly, was compelled to introduce Catholic emancipation after it became clear that Roman Catholics would be elected as MPs in Irish constituencies, though they were not allowed to sit in the House of Commons. George IV was even more reluctant, but had to recognize that Wellington was clearly in charge.

George, both as Regent and King, was very sensitive to criticism. In 1812, when he became Prince Regent, Leigh Hunt launched a savage attack in *The Examiner*.

> The Adonis of Loveliness was a corpulent gentleman of fifty! In short this delightful, blissful, wise, pleasurable, honourable, virtuous, true and immortal Prince was a violator of his word, a libertine over head and ears in debt and disgrace, a despiser of domestic ties, the companion of gamblers and demireps, a man who has just closed half a century without one single claim on the gratitude of his country or the respect of posterity.

George frequently urged the Attorney General of the day to prosecute libellous writers and caricaturists. Few prosecutions followed, since it was discovered that London juries were reluctant to convict. But in this case, Leigh Hunt was arrested and charged with 'An intention to traduce and vilify His Royal Highness'. Despite a spirited defence by Brougham, he was found guilty, fined £500 and sentenced to two years' imprisonment. Shelley was furious that his friend Leigh Hunt had been imprisoned and condemned the Regent as 'a crowned coward and villain'. And what did he want all the money for? 'For supplying the Augean Stable with filth which no second Hercules could cleanse.'

As far as caricatures were concerned, George had tried to stop the most scurrilous either by threatening the cartoonists with prosecution or, when this failed, by bribing them, or by sending his servants out to buy as many copies of the prints as possible so that they could be destroyed. George was particularly sensitive to the cartoons of William Elmes, Charles Williams, and Robert and George Cruikshank. Williams was paid to suppress some cartoons and in 1819 George Cruikshank, the leading caricaturist of the day, signed a receipt for £100, which is in the Royal Archives at Windsor, 'in consideration for a pledge not to caricature His Majesty in an immoral situation'. In the next year his brother, Robert, signed a receipt for £70 surrendering the copyright of the caricature called *The Dandy Of Sixty*. What made these payments so important was that in 1819 there had been a steep rise in the circulation of material attacking the King and the Government.

William Hone, a radical publisher, produced pamphlets with woodcuts by George Cruikshank alongside the text. Hitherto the individual prints produced by the printsellers had sold a few hundred copies, principally in London. Suddenly, there appeared twenty- or thirty-page pamphlets which were very readable, had lots of illustrations and sold in huge quantities. The most popular pamphlet was *The Political House That Jack Built*, which was a sustained attack upon the Government and the King. It certainly helped to inflame the radical and revolutionary sentiments of that year.

The woodcuts were made from boxwood and Cruikshank dubbed them 'Gunpowder in boxwood'. In 1824 Hone claimed that 'they created a new era in the history of publication. They are the parents of the present cheap literature which extends to a sale of at least 400,000 copies every week.'

As late as 1823, George complained about the prints in shop

windows, which portrayed him 'in some ridiculous manner'. But in fact the venom was beginning to die out, for even he benefited from the change of attitude that usually occurred when an heir succeeded to the throne. He was also assisted by a change in fashion. Caricaturists realized there was more money to be made in illustrating books than producing individual prints. George Cruikshank became the leading book illustrator of the Victorian period, being particularly remembered for his illustrations to *Oliver Twist*.

The last years of George IV were sad and unhappy. He had become very gouty and limped heavily. Ramps had to be built in his various houses and he had to be hoisted into chairs. At Windsor he found it easier to abandon his corsets and wore flamboyant and embroidered dressing gowns. George had become something of a recluse: not enjoying going out and meeting the public. He made changes to all his residences to keep out the peeping public eye.

George could not stifle his gargantuan appetite. Wellington records on 9 April 1830 that the King had for breakfast: 'a pigeon and beefsteak pie, of which he ate two pigeons and three beef steaks, three parts of a bottle of Moselle, a glass of dry champagne, two glasses of port and a glass of brandy. He had taken laudanum the night before, again before this breakfast.'

Much of his time was spent by being fortified by cherry brandy and laudanum. He became blind in one eye and he could not sleep lying down, having to sit in an armchair resting his head on a table. In the early hours of 26 June 1830, he died sitting in his chair. He was accompanied by an old friend, Sir Wathen Waller, who was holding his hand. George knew that he was dying. He looked Waller straight in the face and said, 'My dear boy! This is death!'

Apart from the Duke of Clarence, George IV had four other brothers: the Duke of Kent, who was father to Princess Victoria; the Duke of Sussex; the Duke of York; and the Duke of Cumberland. After Charlotte's death they all set about trying to find wives. There were proposals to increase the amounts paid to them by Parliament. Wellington said of them, 'They are the damnedest millstone about the necks of any government that can be imagined. They have insulted – personally insulted – two thirds of the gentlemen of England. How can it be wondered that they take their revenge upon them when they get them in the House of Commons. It is their only opportunity, and I think, by God, they are quite right to use it.'

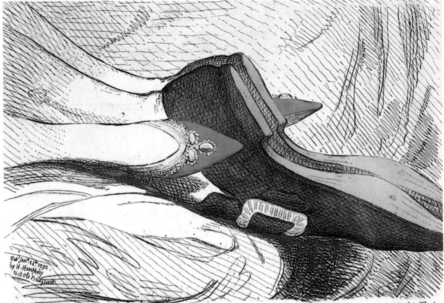

FASHIONABLE CONTRASTS; – or – The Duchess's little Shoe yeilding to the Magnitude of the Duke's Foot.

FASHIONABLE CONTRASTS OR THE DUCHESS'S LITTLE SHOE YIELDING TO THE MAGNITUDE OF THE DUKE'S FOOT, 1792

The Duke of York was George III's second son and to relieve the burden of his debts, he married in 1790 Princess Frederica, a daughter of William II of Prussia. She was very small, not pretty and had bad breath. Her feet only measured 5½ inches and the Duke arranged with the royal shoemaker in London to make her six pairs. News of this got out and so the Princess's shoes feature in many cartoons.

BURNING BY CONTRACT, 1809

*M*rs Clarke knew she was on to a good thing and offered her letters to the press, together with letters written to her by the Duke of York. £10,000 bought her silence, together with an annuity of £400 a year which the Duke had foolishly not cancelled a year earlier. The publisher, Phillips, assures the Chancellor of the Exchequer that 'all is burnt', while hanging from the tails of his coat are papers which read 'a few stories of Mrs Clarke's life for private use'. Plus ça change.

VOICE FROM THE GRAVES, 1830

*T*he Duke of Cumberland, another son of George III, is faced by the ghost of Lord Graves, who had cut his throat after receiving caricatures through the post alleging that his wife was having an affair with Cumberland. The second ghost is Cumberland's former valet, Sellis. In 1809 the Duke claimed that after he had been awakened one night by a murderous attack he had staggered into his valet's room and discovered that Sellis had cut his own throat. Although the jury returned a verdict of suicide, it was widely believed the Cumberland had killed Sellis after being discovered in bed with Sellis's wife. There is an

alleged confession by Cumberland in the royal archives. He may well have been the only member of the modern Royal Family to have actually killed someone with his own hands.

5 · William IV

1830–1837

'A very decent king, but he exhibits oddities'
Charles Greville

WILLIAM, the third son of George III, was born in 1765. At the age of thirteen, he was sent to sea as a midshipman, and by the age of twenty he was a captain. After being present at a naval engagement, it was fleetingly thought that he was destined to be a great admiral. But he won neither the love of his men, nor the respect of his fellow officers.

Returning to England in 1789, William was made the Duke of Clarence; he abandoned any pretensions to a naval career. He had the glamorous status of being a Prince of the royal blood, but he had nothing to do, and very little money. His brother, George, the Prince of Wales, was heavily in debt. William hit upon a plan by which he would marry an heiress and use her money to pay off both their debts. George laughed at this and said to his ungainly brother, 'Who would marry you?'

In 1790, William visited Drury Lane many times and was captivated by the actress Dora Jordan. In the late 18th Century, going to the theatre was the most popular form of communal entertainment. George III and his wife, Queen Charlotte, regularly visited Drury Lane, as did their children. It was rebuilt to accommodate an audience of 3,600. Dora Jordan and Sarah Siddons were the two great actresses who drew the crowds to Drury Lane.

In 1791, William and Dora started to live together in a house at Petersham near Richmond. He was twenty-six years old and passionately in love, but he also had a yearning for domestic affection and comfort. Although William paid her £840 a year, Dora continued to appear at Drury Lane, and in most years earned significantly more than he did. A contemporary satirist wrote:

> *As Jordan's high and mighty Squire*
> *Her playhouse profits deigns to skim,*
> *Some folks audaciously enquire*
> *If he keeps her, or she keeps him.*

THE LUBBER'S-HOLE – ALIAS THE CRACK'D JORDAN, 1791

'*Jordan*' *was the common name for the chamber pot; Gillray uses this as a visual pun showing the Duke of Clarence entering his mistress, Dora Jordan. The print was sold on the streets of London while she was appearing at Drury Lane.*

Dora Jordan had started as an actress in Ireland, where she had the first of her illegitimate children. In 1781, she crossed to England and one of her actor-managers changed her name from Bland to Jordan because, like the Israelites, she had crossed a sea from slavery to freedom. After touring the provinces in Yorkshire, she arrived in London in 1786 and within five years became the star attraction at Drury Lane.

They were eventually to live together for twenty years at Hampton Court, in Bushey House, given to them by George III, during which time she bore him ten children, who were given the name Fitzclarence. It is remarkable, therefore, that she managed to maintain her career as an actress, even playing Ophelia when she was heavily pregnant. But she remained the darling of the boards, and like all great artistes, she loved an audience. William Hazlitt wrote of her, 'She rioted in fine animal spirits . . . She was Cleopatra turned into an oyster-wench, without knowing that she was Cleopatra, or caring that she was an oyster-wench.'

WOUSKI, 1788

The dusky Wouski was a character in a contemporary opera. Prince William had pledged to his father that he would never succumb to the temptations of the fair: but this cartoon suggests how he kept his word.

In 1786, William returned from Jamaica with his ship, and was remarkably frank in expressing his delight in fornication rather than navigation. He had complained to his brother earlier that he had been 'forced to perform with a lady of the town against a wall, or in the middle of a parade'. On another occasion, a fellow-officer had noted that he did not over-indulge in drink, but he would 'go into any house where he saw a pretty girl, and was perfectly acquainted with every house of a certain description in the town'.

THE DEVIL TO PAY: THE WIFE METAMORPHOS'D, OR NEPTUNE REPOSING AFTER FORDING THE JORDAN, 1792

William's uniform is on the back of the chair and Mrs Jordan's stays are on the table as they lie in bed together. All her charms are on display and there is no hint of caricature or distortion, for Gillray wanted to emphasize her beauty. She was short, with masses of curly hair, and she had a good figure with particularly slender legs. Her fine singing voice made her a celebrated comedienne and the toast of London. The young bucks at White's Club presented her with a purse containing £300. She was so popular that she was painted by George Romney, Sir William Beechey and John Hoppner.

Under the bed is the chamber pot bearing the unkind description, 'Public Jordan open to all Parties'. She appears not to mind the insult, for she ends her little reverie with the words, 'Sure I died last night and went to heaven and this is it.'

By 1811, Dora Jordan was fifty and William in his mid-forties: he had tired of her. Deciding that he had to find an heiress – but none would have him – he callously prepared to abandon the woman who had been in effect his wife for twenty years. A formal separation settlement was drawn up. She was given some money, and the children provided for, but she was obliged to forego acting. She also had to hand over her children to him when they reached the age of thirteen, because an actress was considered unsuitable to be a guardian. This was incredibly cruel and insensitive, and for the third time in her life, Dora Jordan was abandoned by the man with whom she had lived.

*George Cruikshank portrays
William, Duke of Clarence, as a
knock-kneed, malignant and
constipated figure. Cruikshank had
been accused by Lord Denham, in the
Queen Caroline Court Case, of 'daily
circulating the most odious and
atrocious calumnies against Her
Majesty'. Denham went on, 'The
Queen could well say, "Come forth
thou slanderer, and let me see thy
face"'.*

After the separation settlement, rumours circulated that there were
terms requiring her to repay money. She still had sufficient wit to send
her former royal lover a playbill with this notice: 'Positively No Money
Refunded After The Curtain Has Risen'. Within two years, Mrs Jordan
decided to go back to the theatre. She was rapturously received. She
was then persuaded to go to France, where she lived a lonely life outside
Paris. When she died a year later in 1816, not one member of her huge
family was with her.

In 1817, following the death of the Prince of Wales's eldest daughter, Princess Charlotte, William decided that he had to marry and try
to produce a legitimate heir. Accordingly, in 1818, he married Princess
Adelaide of Saxe-Meiningen. Their two daughters died in infancy.

There was no love lost between George IV and William. At the
beginning of George's reign the brother who was most likely to succeed
to the throne was William's elder brother, the Duke of York. But when
William became the heir, George remarked to Madame de Lieven, who
was dining at a large banquet in Windsor, 'Look at that idiot – like a
frog's head carved on a coconut. They will remember me if he is ever
in my place.'

William did fill his brother's place in 1830. The diarist Greville
commented, 'A kind-hearted, well-meaning, not stupid, burlesque,
bustling old fellow, and if he doesn't go mad may make a very decent
king, but he exhibits oddities'. William was certainly eccentric. He

THE NEW MASTER, 1830

William IV, plainly dressed, sends Lady Conygnham, his brother's last mistress, and her husband, packing. As soon as George was dead, the Conynghams loaded up wagons with furniture, clocks, valuables, plate and jewels, and carted them off. Between 1821 and 1829, George IV had spent £105,000 on jewels for Lady Conyngham. When William became King, he did not indulge in any extramarital relationships: Queen Adelaide satisfied his flagging appetite.

liked to wander around the streets by himself and once had to be rescued from an over-friendly mob after being kissed by a streetwalker. He was bluff and liked the title, 'The Sailor King'.

William was, however, immediately plunged into a political crisis that was to be much graver than any faced by his successor, Queen Victoria, in her long reign. The General Election that always took place on the accession of a new sovereign led to the Whigs, under Grey, improving their vote, but it still left the Tory Wellington as Prime Minister. The Tories had been deeply divided when Wellington brought in a measure of Catholic emancipation in 1829. This had seemed to the right wing the ultimate abandonment of principle. Wellington therefore had to appease this element in the Party, and in November 1830 he announced that he was implacably opposed to Parliamentary reform. But as the momentum for Reform was there, he in effect precipitated his own resignation.

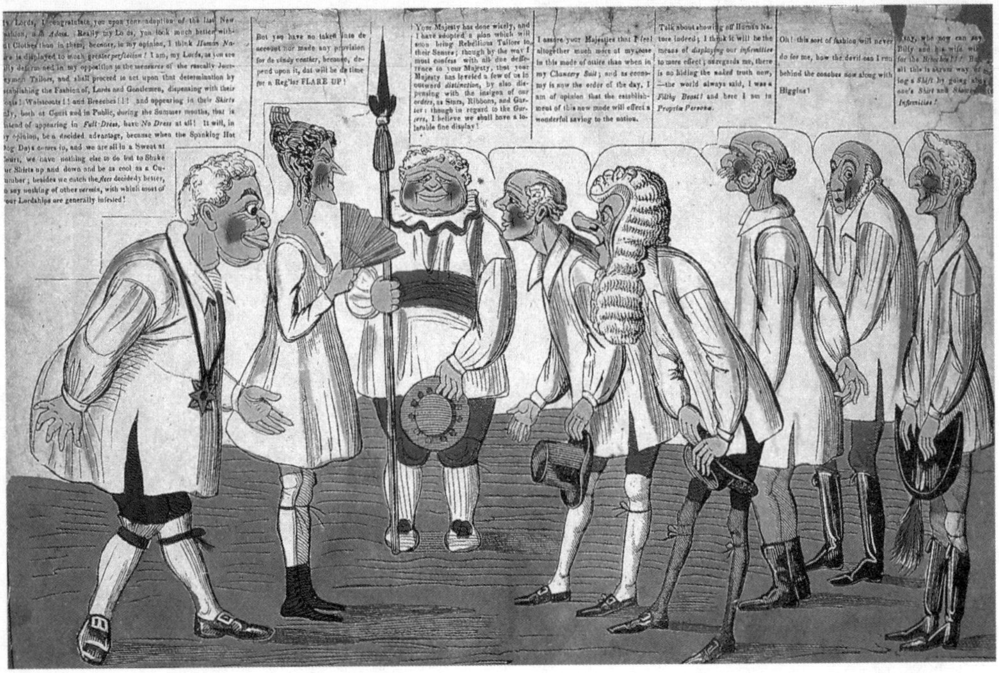

THE LAST NEW FASHION, 1830

William IV had little enthusiasm for Reform, and his Queen, Adelaide, even less. In this woodcut, C. J. Grant, the radical cartoonist, emphasizes the angular face of the Queen, whom he calls 'Queen Addle Head'. Among the most vigorous supporters of Reform were the journeymen tailors of London and here William IV decides to punish them by making the peers give up their coats, waistcoats and breeches in a foolhardy attempt to ruin tailors by establishing a new fashion. This cartoon, which shows the King, the Queen and some peers in various stages of undress, suggests the fatuity of being anti-Reform. Only Wellington, on the right, smiles.

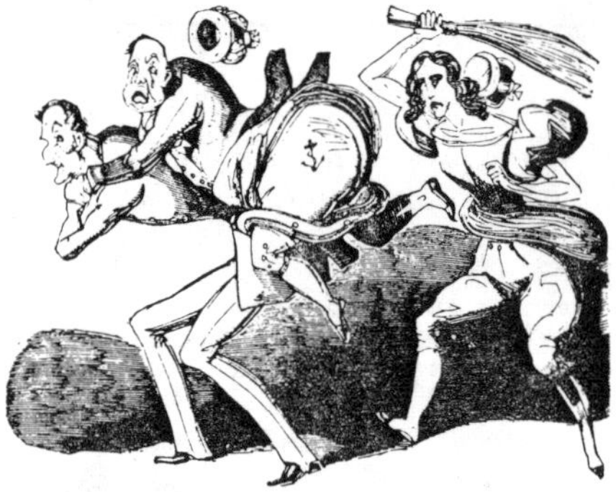

A GERMAN GOVERNESS, 1831

This woodcut reverts to the earlier vigorous style of caricature. Queen Adelaide wears the breeches and birches William, who is supported by Wellington. It is widely thought that Queen Adelaide had stiffened up her husband's opposition to Reform. At the height of the Reform crisis, radical papers hinted at republicanism and spoke of the King and Queen as Mr and Mrs Guelph.

A MUTINY, 1831

*A*n anti-Reform cartoon, in which
the Reformers are cast as
mutineers who have bound and gagged
the King along with the Tory leaders,
Wellington and Peel. The ballast being
tipped out of the boat by Lord John
Russell is honours and decorations.
Later, the Reformers were to get
William to agree to use his power to
create peers to provide a pro-Reform
majority in the House of Lords, if it
proved to be necessary.

Most cartoons, both from the
Reform and anti-Reform sides, show
the King as a sympathizer of their own
side. There was a large body of opinion
that was not too deeply committed
either way but that was likely to be
influenced by the known, or believed,
views of the King.

In 1831 Grey immediately brought forward a Reform Bill to abolish
many rotten boroughs and to increase the size of the electorate, in particular, to bring in many new voters from the growing industrial cities.
When the Bill was defeated, William IV accepted the advice of Grey to
hold a General Election. The Whigs won a substantial majority and
another Bill was passed in the Commons but was strongly opposed in
the Lords. William was told of a plan to create, if necessary, sufficient
ministerial peers to swamp the Opposition, but as the Bill got steadily
into more trouble in the House of Lords he jibbed at creating as many
peers as were going to be needed. Grey resigned, but Wellington could
not form a Government and so William had to accept Grey as Prime

THE PETITION, 1831

A rather unusual example of a cartoon from the anti-Reform side, sharply critical of William IV. The Lord Chancellor, Brougham, presents the King with a petition to release the inmates of three famous lunatic asylums. One of the asylums is shown in the background, the portico of Bedlam, now the Imperial War Museum. The King wears a fool's cap with French Revolutionary additions.

The King is being criticized for being too compliant with the other measures of reform which the Whigs brought forward after the Reform Bill had become law. These measures incurred a great deal of hostility from a nation slow to change.

Minister again. This time he had to agree, without any let-out, to create however many peers were necessary. In effect, the King could not resist the wishes of his Prime Minister, who was supported by a majority in the House of Commons. William realized that the game was up, and he then exerted as much influence as he could to persuade the peers to support the Bill.

The reign of William IV continued the decline in the monarch's powers. In the 18th and early 19th Centuries, it was never envisaged that a King would be told by his Prime Minister exactly how he should use his prerogative in the appointment of peers. Now William could not wriggle out of it and the prerogative powers of the crown were clearly in commission to his leading Minister.

The settlement of 1688, following the expulsion of the Catholic James II, had virtually divided power between the sovereign and the territorial aristocracy. A dynasty cleverer than the Hanoverians might have retained for much longer a greater share of power in the monarch's hands. Whether this would have been a good thing is quite another question. During the whole period, the House of Commons was steadily increasing its influence. Both Walpole and Pitt the Younger knew that their grip on power depended upon creating majorities to carry their Bills in the House of Commons. The Reform Bill of 1832 consolidated this shift in the balance of power. It is just as well that Britain did not have a monarchy determined to defend to the last ditch its prerogatives and powers against the wishes of the people. Somehow Britain had stumbled into a better way of doing things, and avoided another revolution as well.

A GAME AT CHESS, 1832

After Wellington had failed to form a Government in May, William IV recognized the inevitable: 'I don't know how to move, the game is yours.'

William did not like the Whigs, but Grey was their acceptable face. He was a landed aristocrat who presented reform to the King as a necessary measure to preserve the monarchy and the aristocracy in the new era.

6 · Victoria

1837–1901

"Ave you 'eard o' the Widow at Windsor
With a hairy gold crown on 'er head?'
Rudyard Kipling, *The Widow at Windsor*

QUEEN Victoria's long reign falls into three parts. The first was from 1837 to 1861 – the death of her husband, Albert; the second from 1861 to about 1876 – the 'Widow at Windsor' period; and the third from 1876 to 1901, during which she became the mother figure of the nation and Empire, and the most famous person in the world.

Victoria was born in 1819, the only child of the fourth son of George III, the Duke of Kent, who died a few months after her birth. It was by no means certain that she would succeed to the throne. Her aunt, Adelaide, the wife of the Duke of Clarence, later William IV, tried to produce an heir, but her children died shortly after their birth. But even as late as 1835 it was thought that Adelaide was pregnant. William, therefore, was reluctant to recognize Victoria as the likely successor, though it became progressively more likely through his reign that she would succeed.

Victoria was brought up by her mother, the Duchess of Kent, and was not allowed to mix with children of her own age. The Duchess tried to ensure that she would have influence over her daughter when she became Queen. She intrigued with her Private Secretary, Sir John Conroy, to achieve this. Victoria, from the start, was determined to show she was in charge. When she became Queen, her mother was pushed into the background; Conroy was not granted an audience; and even her old companion, Letzen, was eventually pensioned off.

Victoria's accession really saved the monarchy. If her other uncle, Cumberland, or someone in the mould of George IV had succeeded, then a call for a different system of appointing a head of state would have resounded throughout the land. Victoria's great advantage was that she was a total contrast, and the nation rejoiced in a fresh start. The aura was reinforced by the fact that she was an innocent young virgin. She recorded in her diary, for she was a voluminous diarist, the

A SCENE IN THE NEW FARCE CALLED 'THE RIVALS', 1819

*T*his print could claim to be the first picture of Victoria, as she is in her mother's womb. The heavily pregnant Duchess of Kent is seen with her husband standing behind. All the Royal uncles – the Duke and Duchess of Clarence, later William IV, on the left; the Duke of Cambridge and his wife, seated in the centre; and the Duke and Duchess of Cumberland on the right – set about trying to produce an heir following the death of Princess Charlotte. William and Adelaide's children died in infancy, and the little baby in this print became the gruff Duke of Cambridge, Commander-in-Chief of the Army. He did not succeed, because his father was the younger brother of the Duke of Kent. It was little Victoria who won the jackpot in this lottery.

news of her accession. On the morning of 20 June, she was woken at 6 o'clock by her mother and told that the Archbishop of Canterbury was waiting to see her: 'I got out of bed and went into my sitting room (only in my dressing gown) and *alone* and saw them. Lord Conyngham, the Lord Chamberlain, then acquainted me that my poor Uncle, the King, was no more and had expired at 12 minutes past two this morning and consequently that I am the *Queen*.' The myth machine was soon in action and a famous painting of this scene captured her description in a very romantic way.

DESIGN FOR A REGENCY, 1830

As heir to the throne, the little Princess Victoria had become an important property; many people vied to control her. Her mother, the Duchess of Kent, won; here she is holding the Orb while sitting on the throne. But she is not very happy with her brother Leopold playing Bob Cherry with the young Victoria. In this game the player attempts to grasp a suspended cherry – here meaning royal powers – between her teeth. In the following year, Leopold became King of the Belgians and Victoria sought his advice frequently. In the Council Chamber on the right, Wellington, the Prime Minister, presides in the royal chair, with the Grenadier Guards holding fixed bayonets behind him. William IV had virtually no control over the upbringing of Victoria.

VICTORIA'S BIRTHDAY, 1837

Figaro in London *records the scene on 24 May 1837 when Victoria reached the age of 18. A Regent would no longer be required. William IV told her that he would ask Parliament to grant her £10,000 to be entirely at her disposal, and she could appoint her own officials. Her mother had been named as Regent, if the office were to become necessary, and her Private Secretary, Sir John Conroy, loathed by virtually everybody, had intrigued to get real control over Victoria. When she*

became Queen a few weeks later, she refused to see Conroy and she slowly reduced her mother's influence, although the Duchess did have rooms in Buckingham Palace until her daughter's marriage to Albert in 1840.

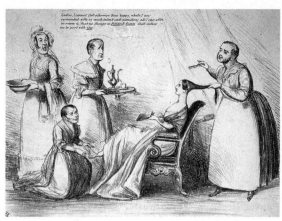

LADIES OF THE BEDCHAMBER, 1839

THE SOVEREIGN LED BY HER MINISTERS, 1839

*T*he Prime Minister, Melbourne, took over the Queen, a point publicly acknowledged in Figaro in London. He coached her in making speeches; dined with her two or three times a week; and, as she enjoyed riding, went out with her frequently. They also did jigsaw puzzles together. She looked upon him as her father and he educated her politically. The Duchess of Kent wrote to her daughter, 'Take care that Lord Melbourne is not King.' In the 1840s, Victoria lent Melbourne money from her own account, when he ran into financial difficulties, recalling her grandfather, George III, who had lent money to Lord North to pay his debts when he was actually Prime Minister.

*T*he Bedchamber Crisis occurred in May 1839. When Melbourne's majority was steadily eroded in the House of Commons, he resigned – an act which produced floods of tears from Victoria. He advised her to call Peel, not Wellington, who was too old. Peel was concerned that the Ladies of the Royal Household around Victoria all had husbands who, as they were Whigs, would influence her against his advice. He asked Victoria to change some of her Ladies. When she absolutely refused to do so, the issue became the sticking point. Melbourne, behind the scenes, had been encouraging Victoria to believe that this was an essential power for the sovereign to retain. In the cartoon the Whigs, Melbourne and Russell, turn to the Queen, who says: 'No change in political events shall induce me to part with you.'

After four days, Peel realized that he could not form a Government. This was the last occasion that a monarch exerted personal wishes to produce a change of Prime Minister. The whole crisis was a Pyrrhic victory: within a few years the monarchy's control over appointing the Officers of the Royal Household was removed.

THE GRAND RANGER AND HIS PET DEER, 1839

*A*lbert had been picked out years earlier as the husband of the future Queen of England and he devoted his career to achieving that aim. He arrived in England on 10 October 1839 and the young Victoria fell head over heels in love with him. She wrote: 'Albert really is quite charming and so excessively handsome, such beautiful blue eyes, an exquisite nose and such a pretty mouth and delicate mustachios, slight but very slight whiskers; a beautiful figure, broad in the shoulders and a fine waist; my heart is quite going.' Within four days she had proposed to him. Later she made him the Ranger of Richmond Park, a post that carried an elaborate uniform which Albert liked to wear. They were married in February 1840.

TENDER ANNUALS, 1843

*V*ictoria and Albert's first child, Princess Victoria, who was to be the mother of the Kaiser, was born in October 1840. Edward, Prince of Wales, was born in March 1841 – the first male heir to be born to the family for nearly 80 years. In all, Victoria had nine children. Although she dreaded pregnancy and confinement, she none the less believed that it was her duty to bear Albert's children. In this cartoon, John Bull is aghast at the cost to the taxpayer of just three children and says, 'I shall have such a stock of them sort o'plants on my hands I shan't know what to do with them.'

LIGHT SOVEREIGNS, 1843

This cartoon demonstrates the power of Britain in Europe in the early years of Victoria's reign. The young Queen outweighs the crowned heads of Europe. It was to be Britain's century.

The monarchs in the front row on the scales are Louis Philippe of France, Ernest Augustus of Hanover and Tsar Nicholas I of Russia. To the right is Leopold I of the Belgians, and at the back is the Emperor Ferdinand of Austria. The French, Russian and Austrian sovereigns were more important, but Ernest and Leopold were Victoria's relatives.

The change in the character of the monarchy chimed with a change of feelings and sentiments in the country. The Reform Bill debates of 1830–32 had created a new style of politics – where issues were as important as personalities. The end of the period of Regency indulgence saw the emergence of a new high-seriousness, which infused public debate and determined personal behaviour.

Victoria was inexperienced in the arts of politics and made some early blunders over the Bedchamber Crisis, in which Peel attempted to remove Whig influence from her household, and the associated campaign against one of her ladies-in-waiting. But she learnt quickly from Melbourne, her first Prime Minister, whom she looked upon as a father figure as well as a political and constitutional mentor. In 1840 she married Prince Albert of Saxe-Coburg and became a devoted wife. She bore him nine children, and for much of the 1840s and 1850s she was the Queen Pregnant as well as the Queen Regnant. This preoccupation with her family allowed Albert to become her Private Secretary, filtering her papers, sometimes summarizing and commenting upon them. They discussed everything together, from state affairs to a new dress.

Albert had some remarkable qualities – he was well educated, with a genuine interest in the arts and sciences; he had an immense capacity

TELL ME, OH TELL ME, DEAREST ALBERT, HAVE YOU ANY RAILWAY SHARES? 1845

*T*he 1840s saw heavy investment in the railways and a huge speculative rise in railway shares. George Hudson, the railway king, gave away shares to members of the old nobility in an attempt to add respectability to his speculative ventures. There was no evidence that Albert invested, but many did – and suffered huge losses when the bubble burst.

Victoria was the most financially prudent monarch to sit upon the throne of England. She paid off her father's debts and she husbanded her resources and those of her family very well. In 1837 she had a vote from Parliament of £385,000 a year and this was not increased during her reign. In addition, she had incomes from the Duchies of Cornwall and Lancaster amounting to £27,000. She became a very rich woman. She was left a legacy of £250,000 by an eccentric recluse in the 1850s. Although she was accompanied by a huge entourage of servants and staff wherever she went, she did not spend her money rashly. Typically, when she set out for the Golden Jubilee procession in 1887 she decided to wear her second-best hat, which had been bought from a Windsor draper.

ROYAL PRIVACY IN THE HIGHLANDS, 1848

*V*ictoria and Albert visited Scotland first in 1842, travelling there by sea. They both fell in love with it and returned in 1844, 1847 and 1848. Victoria was the first English monarch, not born in Scotland, who really liked the country. She said, 'She is the brightest jewel in my crown.' In 1847, Victoria and Albert acquired first the leasehold and then the freehold of the Balmoral Estate for 30,000 guineas. Albert set about rebuilding the house in a mixture of Scottish baronial and French renaissance styles; he also designed the Balmoral tartan.

Victoria liked Balmoral very much because it was one of the driest places in Scotland. But she particularly favoured the isolation and the privacy that the estate gave. The press, however, even in those days was always trying to find details about how the Royal Family lived. In this cartoon (opposite, above), *which appeared in a magazine called* The Puppet Show, *investigative reporters of the day from the* Morning Post, The Times, Morning Herald *and* Daily News *would not leave them alone.*

Victoria spent seven years of her life at Balmoral. Her first published work in 1867 was Leaves from a journal of our Life in the Highlands. *This allowed Disraeli to say to Victoria, 'We authors, ma'am.' The book sold 20,000 copies overnight.*

for engrossing himself in detailed work; and he was the most intellectual of all the Hanoverian brood. He was a high-minded man for a high-minded age. The biggest project with which he was involved was the Great Exhibition of 1851; with his restless energy, he pushed it forward. He ensured that it left behind some significant memorials in the shape of the South Kensington Museum complex, Imperial College and the Royal College of Art. He was granted the title of Prince Consort in 1857, though Victoria had toyed with the idea of making him 'King', an idea which found no favour with any of her Ministers. Being Consort was not a real job.

In fact, Albert was not very popular and some never allowed him to forget his German origin. One of the street songs at the time of his marriage emphasized that he was both German and poor, and that John Bull would have to foot the bill for his children. He also had strong views on politics, supporting Peel's reforms and trying to soften Palmerston's aggressive nationalism. His health broke down in the 1850s and he died at the age of 42, literally worn out, since his frame could not resist the onset of typhoid fever. Victoria had come to count upon him completely: in 1848 she had told her Uncle Leopold that she could not 'exist' without Albert. After his death, she turned him into a saint and all her children were made to worship at the shrine. Nevertheless, by the end of her reign he was a largely forgotten figure from a distant age.

O GOD OF BATTLES!, 1857

The first news of the Indian Mutiny reached Britain in 1857. The whole country was shocked to learn that when the garrison at Cawnpore fell, the women and children had their throats cut. The Queen wrote of this massacre: 'the horrors committed on the poor ladies – women and children – are unknown in these ages and makes one's blood run cold ... There is not a family hardly who is not in sorrow and anxiety about their children.'

Here Victoria is portrayed as the mother of her people, comforting but resilient. It was a relatively new role for the sovereign and it was to be developed by several of the Queen's descendants.

A FRENCH LESSON, 1871

Republicanism was given a boost not only by Victoria's seclusion, but also by the Prince of Wales's behaviour. The Queen stayed at home too much and the Prince of Wales stayed at home too little. Republican clubs sprang up in London, Birmingham, Aberdeen, Cardiff and Plymouth. A prominent Liberal MP, Charles Dilke, attacked the Civil List and claimed that 'a republic here will be free from this political corruption that hangs about the monarchy'. Punch, in one of its 'speaking for the nation' moods, published this cartoon by Sir John Tenniel, which shows the consequences of republicanism in France where, following the deposition of Napoleon III, the Paris Commune had plunged the city into vicious revolutionary excess.

The year 1867 saw the first publication of a radical magazine called Tomahawk, *whose leading cartoonist was Matt Morgan. His most famous cartoon was the empty throne draped with a cover to resemble furniture in an empty house. Following Albert's death in 1861, Victoria had become a recluse – the widow of Windsor – spending her time at Windsor, Osborne and Balmoral, and not even bothering to attend the opening of Parliament. She whinged to one of her Prime Ministers, Lord John Russell, that the public desire to 'witness the spectacle of a poor broken-hearted widow, nervous and shrinking, dragged in deep mourning, ALONE in a STATE as a Show, where she used to go supported by her husband, to be gazed at without delicacy or feeling, is a thing she cannot understand and she could never wish her bitterest foe to be exposed to'. Republicanism was given a boost by her neglect of the outward signs of royalty.*

After Albert's death, Victoria became a recluse, reluctant even to fulfil official royal engagements. Her seclusion in Windsor, Balmoral and Osborne spurred republicanism. In the 1870s the popular press and satirical pamphlets talked freely of abdication. When Disraeli became Prime Minister in 1874, he decided to bring the Queen back into public life. She appealed to his romantic temperament and he even invested her with the aura of the Faery. He poured on her buckets of flattery and made her the Empress of India in 1876. She favoured him by resuming the habit of opening Parliament – she opened three Parliaments for Disraeli, but only one for Gladstone.

THANKSGIVING, 1872

*R*epublicanism was stemmed by an
extraordinary turn of events. In the
winter of 1871, almost exactly ten
years after the death of the Prince
Consort, Edward contracted typhoid
fever, the very disease from which his
father had died, and at one time he was
given up for dead. Bulletins were
issued, sometimes as many as five a
day, to tell the public about his illness.
The future Poet Laureate, Alfred
Austin, composed the memorable lines:

> Across the wires the electric message
> came
> He is no better, he is much the same.

There was a thanksgiving service in St
Paul's to celebrate his recovery, and the
Queen was persuaded to sit beside the
Prince in the carriage leading the
procession. As the London crowds
cheered and cheered, the Queen came
to realize that appearing in public was
not so much an ordeal as a necessary
aspect of modern monarchy.

In the last 25 years of her reign, the monarchy became widely loved and
respected as a symbol of Britain's greatness. This short, stout woman,
dressed invariably in black, who spoke with a guttural German accent,
became the mother figure of the largest empire the world had ever seen.
This was the foundation of the modern monarchy. Ceremony became
an important part of the mystique. Although the royal weddings were
family affairs, they became the subject of widespread interest; the illus-
trated magazines were full of detailed family trees showing the
immense complexity of the inter-relationships of her brood. The two
most powerful sovereigns in Europe were her relations: Kaiser Wilhelm
II of Germany was her grandson and was at her bedside when she died,
and Tsar Nicholas II of Russia married one of her granddaughters.
Victoria spent much of her time looking after and promoting the interests of her family – family life was certainly a Victorian value.

THE SWEET ROSE AND THE PRICKLY THISTLE, 1876

*T*his cartoon appeared in a series of
satirical poems which attacked the
Queen and the Prince of Wales. It hints
at the sinister influence that John
Brown, who had been appointed a
ghillie in 1855, was supposed to have
over the Queen. In 1872 he became her
personal attendant, for she liked his
brusque manner: he addressed her as
'Wumman'. In France it was thought
that she was his mistress. She
overlooked his fondness for whisky, but
in 1883 he was to die from delirium
tremens.

EMPRESS AND EARL, 1876

*D*israeli became Prime Minister in
1874 and immediately set about
bringing the Queen back into public
life. In a romantic gesture, not entirely
devoid of Realpolitik, he made her the
Empress of India in 1876 and she
reciprocated by making him an Earl.
Disraeli recognized the importance of
buttering-up the queen: 'You have
heard me called a flatterer, and it is
true. Everyone likes flattery and when
it comes to royalty you should lay it on
with a trowel.' He said of his
relationship with her: 'I never deny; I
never contradict; I sometimes forget.'
On another occasion, he observed:
'Gladstone treats the Queen like a
public department; I treat her like a
woman.' He was her favourite Prime
Minister and she sent primroses, the
flowers which he used to give her, to his
grave every year. Victoria was a Whig
under Melbourne, a Peelite under
Albert's influence, but had become a
Conservative under Disraeli.

THE QUEEN AND
HER DOLLS, 1892

Gladstone was Prime Minister four times, but in the latter part of his career he had the worst possible relations with Victoria. In 1885 she had tried to prevent him becoming Prime Minister, saying that she had 'the greatest possible disinclination to take this half-crazy and really in many ways ridiculous old man'. Victoria was spiteful, and in spite of his great age, she never allowed him to sit in her presence. Gladstone declared to Rosebery that, 'The Queen alone is enough to kill any man!'

In this cartoon from Fun *the politician in the jack-in-the-box is Henry Labouchère, a radical liberal and the editor of the magazine,* Truth. *In 1892, Victoria refused to accept Gladstone's suggestion that Labouchère should be a minister, a reminder that the sovereign still retained considerable political influence. She may have recalled Labouchère's parody of the National Anthem:*

> *Grandchildren not a few,*
> *With great-grandchildren too,*
> *She blest has been.*
> *We've been their sureties,*
> *Paid them gratuities,*
> *Pensions, annuities,*
> *God save the Queen!*

THE RARE, THE RATHER AWFUL VISITS OF ALBERT EDWARD, PRINCE OF WALES, TO WINDSOR CASTLE

This famous cartoon by Beerbohm says it all.

SOCIETY'S IDOL 1841: SOCIETY'S IDOL 1891

By 1891 Edward, Prince of Wales, had had to appear twice in two different court actions. One concerned a divorce and the other an allegation of cheating at baccarat against a fellow guest in a country house where he had stayed for the weekend. This shocked late Victorian England. Here (above and above left) he was satirized in Truth. *His lifestyle of gambling, racing, eating and drinking, and his string of mistresses, contrasted sharply with the abstemious behaviour of his mother.*

A JUBILEE REVERIE, 1887

*B*y the mid-1880s, Victoria had become an institution in her own right. She had been the monarch of the most powerful country in the world for nearly fifty years and various members of her vast family were soon to fill the

thrones of other countries. No monarch has ever been so completely associated with the age in which they lived – whether it was the military victories, engineering triumphs, works of literary genius, or even the mugs on people's mantlepieces. All were described as 'Victorian'.

ÉCHOES DU RIRE, c. 1900

*L*e Rire *was a French satirical magazine that was more vigorous and scathing than* Punch *had ever been. Many countries in Europe sympathized with the Boers in the South African war, and Britain was very unpopular. Here the Queen welcomes a visit by the Kaiser, her grandson. But Paul Kruger, President of the Transvaal, is shocked by this apparent friendship, because the Kaiser had supported him in 1896, at the time of the Jameson Raid, in which an attempt was made to dislodge Boer control of the Transvaal. The Kaiser assures him that this is merely a social visit.*

RETOUR D'IRLANDE, 1900

*T*his French postcard comments simply on the Queen's last visit to Ireland. Winston Churchill described the event: 'Prompted by a desire to recognise the gallantry of her Irish soldiers in South Africa, she travelled to Dublin in April 1900, wearing the shamrock on her bonnet and jacket. Her Irish subjects, even the Nationalists among them, gave her a rousing reception. In Ireland a fund of goodwill still flowed for the Throne, on which English Governments sadly failed to draw.'

The Queen rides in an Irish jaunty-cart, drawn by a donkey. In French cartoons, she was often depicted drinking a great deal and, in this case, she is riding on a bottle of gin. There was no evidence in her lifestyle to support the canard.

*M*any late 19th-Century French
cartoons were bitterly critical of
Victoria. She was often portrayed as a
drunk, greedy harridan. In this cartoon
from Le Charivari, her right hand lays
claim to most of Africa, while her left
hand plants the British flag in Asia.
The long rivalry between England and
France in the building of their Empires
still survived, though other countries,
such as Germany and Portugal,
engaged in the scramble for Africa. In
the late 19th Century most people
would have thought that war with
France was more likely than war with
Germany.

Apart from the Crimea there were no great wars involving Britain
in Victoria's reign and so there were no great victory parades. The ceremonies which celebrated her Golden Jubilee in 1887 and her Diamond
Jubilee in 1897 more than made up for this. The streets of London were
full of soldiers who came from all over her Empire to worship the Great
White Queen.

The Queen owed much of her influence to the fact that she was the
head of society – her favour meant recognition and her disfavour seclusion. High society in late Victorian times was a pyramid of formal relationships whose influence spread right throughout the country.
Invested with such reverence, the whole system was directed to please
and to satisfy her whims. Ministers were kept waiting, children and
their parents were suddenly summoned, and only her convenience mat-
tered.

Politically, Victoria's influence was maintained by her sheer
longevity and character. During the period 1846–67, following the collapse of Peel's Tory Party, she had to choose between various Prime
Ministers, one of the few prerogatives left to the crown. She relished it.
She tried to avoid appointing Palmerston in the 1850s and Gladstone in
the 1880s. But she failed. In 1894, following Gladstone's resignation, she
chose Rosebery as the Prime Minister over the much more experienced

Liberal leader, Harcourt, and over Lord Spencer, whom Gladstone would have recommended had he been asked. She also managed to keep the radicals, Sir Charles Dilke and Henry Labouchère, out of office. She could not resist interfering in foreign affairs and publicly condemned Gladstone over his failure to save Gordon at Khartoum. But in fact she had very little influence over many major decisions and she had no interest in the social and industrial problems of the country.

Before Victoria ascended the throne, acid and disrespectful satire had disappeared from caricature. The individual print, run off in the heat of the moment and sold principally to those who lived in Central London, had been succeeded by newspapers and magazines accompanied by woodcuts and later steel engravings. The new, more serious audience was much larger. The father of the household did not want his wife and daughters to see scurrilous and lewd cartoons in his drawing room.

Victoria therefore got off pretty lightly. In the first period she is pictured as the young wife and mother, although Albert gets it in the neck for being German. There were a few weekly periodicals in the 1830s, *The Looking Glass*, *Figaro* and *Cleaves' Penny Gazette*, aimed at the literate and radically minded artisans living in and around London. They faded away, but in 1841 *Punch* appeared for the first time.

It was immensely respectable. For the first few years it supported some radical causes, such as Chartism, but it became in effect the magazine of the Establishment by the Establishment. Only in the 1860s did some rivals begin to appear, *Judy* and *Fun* among them. The one most critical of the Queen was the shortlived *Tomahawk*, which was first published in 1867. This was the low point for the Queen as far as cartoons were concerned. From the 1870s, the cartoonists had another target, the Prince of Wales, and they contrasted his lifestyle with that of the Queen. In the last years of her reign, British cartoons of the Queen were uniformly respectful. Only in French, German and South African periodicals was she attacked.

7 · *Edward VII*

1901–1910

'"God Save Him", they said when he lived, the words now sound odd
For we know that in Heaven above at this moment he is saving God'

Max Beerbohm

Edward had to wait a very long time before he became King. His mother reigned for nearly 64 years – four years longer than George III. Edward commented wryly, 'I don't mind praying to the Eternal Father, but I must be the only man in the country afflicted with an eternal mother.' His long apprenticeship as the Prince of Wales proved that being heir to the throne is virtually a non-job. He undertook regional tours around the country, though he particularly enjoyed travelling abroad as an unofficial ambassador for Britain. He was undoubtedly a helpful presence, but a succession of Foreign Secretaries ensured that he had little or no influence on foreign policy.

Victoria was highly critical of Edward's lifestyle. He would never measure up to her beloved Albert. She was so besotted with Albert that she insisted that all Edward's male children should bear his name; she also wanted him to be crowned Albert I, a proposal which Edward, with some spirit, resisted.

Albert had laid down a rigid daily regime of lessons, designed to improve his son's mind, but Edward, though intelligent, was not remotely intellectual. He had little interest in ideas, art or literature, and the only plays he liked were about high society. He did, however, acquire fluency in French and German. It is remarkable that Edward managed to survive his childhood with his sanity intact.

After Albert's death, Victoria would not involve Edward in the business of running the country. He was allowed to open schools and hospitals, and to attend parades, but he was not allowed to see state papers. He complained to several Prime Ministers about this; only

THE PRINCE, 1871

This flattering cartoon appeared in Vanity Fair and shows Edward in a boating jacket, because he regularly appeared at Cowes.

A WELL-STOCKED NURSERY, 1844

Victoria, and particularly Albert, gave a lot of attention to the education of their children. Albert, unlike his predecessors, actually played with his children – though the Prince of Wales, from the start, was a handful. At the age of four – the time of this cartoon – his teacher reported to the Queen that Edward had 'impetuous spirits' and a liking for 'violent exercise and enjoyment of life'.

Disraeli realized that he needed more, feeding him titbits of information from the Cabinet. It was not until Rosebery became Prime Minister in 1894 that Edward was allowed to have Prince Albert's golden key which opened despatch boxes. Before then he had to ask Cabinet Ministers what had happened at Cabinet.

Edward had quite a problem in filling up his time because he was by nature an energetic man. He visited parts of the Empire that no previous monarch or heir had visited. When it was announced that he would go on a visit to the Middle East in 1868, *Tomahawk*, the radical magazine, criticized him on the grounds that he was needed more at home, since Victoria had become a recluse. Nevertheless, throughout his life he spent between three and four months of the year outside the country.

In March 1863, when twenty-two years old, Edward married Princess Alexandra of Denmark. She was very beautiful but slightly deaf, a hereditary complaint which was to get progressively worse and made her, after a few years, isolated. Like her husband, she was not remotely interested in intellectual matters and between them they

THE ROYAL ROAD TO LEARNING, 1859

Edward wanted to join the Army, but his parents ruled this out. He had a series of personal tutors who struggled to engage his attention. The Queen much preferred his elder sister and wrote to her, 'I feel very sad about him. He is so idle and so weak.' Albert thought his son was 'a thorough and cunning lazybones'. Edward was sent to Edinburgh, Oxford and Cambridge Universities, but he did not become a member of any of the colleges, and this Punch *cartoon shows him being greeted not by fellow students but by obsequious dons. A separate establishment was created, in which he became a private student with specially selected tutors and companions. It was all totally alien to Edward's temperament.*

LATEST FROM AMERICA, 1860

Edward's first official visit to the United States went down very well indeed. He had already started to devote himself to his main pursuit, which was enjoying life, and he was well into cigars and drinking.

Unlike other Princes of Wales, his loss of virginity was well and truly recorded. In 1860, when he was attached to the Grenadier Guards at the Curragh Military camp in Dublin, fellow officers persuaded an actress, Nellie Clifden, to wait for the Prince in his bed. The Prince liked her so much that he continued to see her in London. News of this affair soon reached Prince Albert, who told the Queen; both were appalled.

At that time, Albert was already in poor health, and although exhausted he went to Cambridge to see his son. The Queen felt that Bertie's affair with Nellie precipitated Albert's illness and she said in a letter to her eldest daughter, 'I never can or shall look at him without a shudder as you may imagine.'

barely opened a book a year. Their first son, Albert Eddy, was born in 1864, and the second son, George, later to be George V, in 1865. A daughter followed in 1867, but then Alexandra contracted rheumatic fever which left her with a limp and made her even deafer. There was a fourth child in 1868 and a fifth in 1869, but she lost a sixth in 1871.

Queen Alexandra was more beautiful than any of Edward's mistresses, but her beauty did not stop his compulsive womanizing. In 1877 he started an affair with Lily Langtry, the wife of a Belfast shipbuilder. He took her, quite openly, to Ascot and to dinner at Maxim's in Paris. Of all his affairs this was the most well known because he helped to launch her upon a stage career, where she became known as the Jersey Lily, after the island of her birth.

Edward then fell head-over-heels in love with Daisy Brooke, who was twenty years his junior. She was a leading figure in London society and soon became his mistress, later becoming the Countess of Warwick. Edward would write to her two or three times a week with such endearments as, 'My own lovely little Daisy'. His last great love

L'Impudique Albion

L'Impudique Albion

BARE BOTTOMS, 1901

The three main satirical French magazines, L'Assiette de Beurre, Le Rire *and* Le Charivari *all strongly supported the Boers against the British. Above left is the celebrated back cover* *by Jean Veber for the issue of* L'Assiette de Beurre, *28 September 1901. Edward VII was very offended and threatened to refuse to open an exhibition in Paris. The French authorities demanded that the bottom be covered up and above right is how it appeared in the tenth edition.*

THE TRANBY CROFT AFFAIR, 1890

This drawing of the game of baccarat, in which Gordon-Cumming was accused of cheating, and at which the Prince of Wales was *present and dealing the cards, appeared in Labouchère's magazine* Truth, *just in time for Christmas in 1890. The matter became a court case, tried before the Lord Chief Justice, Lord Coleridge, the following June.*

was Mrs Keppel, whose soldier husband was quite willing to acquiesce in his wife becoming the mistress of the King. As Keppel was rather hard-up, Edward asked his friend, Sir Thomas Lipton, the grocer, to give him a job.

Mrs Keppel became completely involved in his life. She attended his parties at Marlborough House, where she was recognized by the Princess. She even sat next to the Archbishop of Canterbury, who believed that her close relationship with the Princess demonstrated that she could not possibly be the Prince's mistress. She was Edward's last great love. When he was dying, Mrs Keppel showed to Alexandra a letter written a long time before, asking her to be present, and the Queen allowed her to see him just before he died. After his death, Alexandra said, 'He always loved me the best.'

All these women were married, but that did not prevent Edward from seducing them. He arranged for them to be invited to house parties which he was going to attend and where it was accepted that anybody could sleep with somebody's else spouse. Hilaire Belloc wrote some appropriate verses:

> And Mr Hunt, who manufactures soap,
> Will answer for Victoria, Lady Tring,
> And Algernon will partner Mrs Scrope –
> And Mrs James will entertain the King.
>
> There will be bridge and booze till after three
> And, after that, a lot of them will grope
> Along the passage in robes de nuit
> And dressing gowns, in search of other dope.
>
> And a trained nurse will be sent down to cope
> With poor De Vere, who isn't quite the thing,
> And give his wife the signal to elope –
> And Mrs James will entertain the King.

Edward's life was one long round of pleasure – racing, yachting, eating, drinking, shooting, deer-stalking, long weekend parties, balls where he enjoyed dancing, and gambling. His valets took with them Edward's own special counters for gambling; they bore the Prince of Wales's feather. He liked organizing shoots at Sandringham and he proudly recorded the huge battues – 3,000 birds and 6,000 rabbits in a day.

STAR OF INDIA, 1876

The official visit to India was a great success. Edward enjoyed being an unofficial ambassador, a role that he in effect established for the monarchy. In Bombay, lanterns spelt out the message, 'Tell Mamma we're happy.' Certainly Edward was, as he enjoyed shooting tigers and elephants on an imperial scale. Reynolds News was the principal vehicle attacking his lifestyle and it bluntly said that the only things he was interested in were 'women and pig-sticking'.

This journey was famous for a royal innovation. On the boat going out, Edward decreed that tailcoats need not be worn at dinner and he wore a short black coat – the dinner jacket was born. Edward took a great interest in his appearance. He popularized the Norfolk jacket and established the habit of leaving the bottom button of a waistcoat undone – embonpoint had won.

Edward had a trivial mind, loving to play practical jokes. He infuriated his staff by making tiny amendments to the drafts of his speeches. He enjoyed dressing up and was particularly fond of his Field Marshal's uniform. He tried to join the expedition to Egypt in 1882, but the Cabinet would not let him go – for the only battle that he had witnessed was the Battle of Flowers at Cannes.

Apart from gambling and shooting, Edward enjoyed racing and was remarkably successful – winning the Derby in 1896 and again in 1900. He also won the Grand National. Between 1886 and 1910, stud fees and estate money contributed over £400,000, and certainly paid his racing costs. He was the first King to enjoy racing since George, the young Prince of Wales, had given it up after a scandal at Newmarket in the 1780s.

The courtiers and friends of Edward devoted their lives to ensuring that he was provided with endless diversion. He was petulant if he was not pampered and irascible if he was not entertained. Fate had dealt him a good hand and he intended to enjoy it to the full. Edward's circle was fast-moving, very rich and rather louche. The Queen deplored her son spending his time with the 'frivolous, selfish, and pleasure-seeking rich'. It was inevitable that he would be led into public scrapes. The two most prominent scandals were the Mordaunt divorce action of 1870, and the Tranby Croft baccarat scandal in 1891.

In 1870 Edward was cited with others by Sir Charles Mordaunt in a divorce action against his twenty-one-year-old wife. She claimed to have slept with several people, including the Prince of Wales, and there were supposed to be incriminating letters; but when these were revealed they were found to be quite banal. Lady Mordaunt was deranged and eventually committed to a lunatic asylum. However, the Prince did have to appear as a witness in the Court to deny that he had committed any improper act with her. The real humiliation was that the heir to the throne had to go to Court in a case of this sort.

The Tranby Croft Affair was altogether more serious. In September 1890 Edward spent a weekend at the Yorkshire country home of Arthur Wilson, a rich shipowner. The party also included Lieut. Col. Sir

A 'COUNTER' IRRITATION, 1891

The Queen in a letter to her son had said, 'The monarch almost is in danger if he is lowered and despised.' Following pressure from the Queen, Edward wrote a letter to the Archbishop of Canterbury expressing his 'horror of gambling', but to many this seemed to be an act of hypocrisy. Funny Folks depicted him as a naughty boy, scolded by his mother.

CUMMMING DOWN, 1891

During the case that Gordon-Cumming brought to clear his name over Tranby Croft, the public was generally on his side; the Prince of Wales was attacked for his passion for gambling. The Prince attended Court on each day of the trial and had lunch with the Judge, who not surprisingly summed up against Gordon-Cumming – advice that the jury followed. The Prince of Wales was particularly annoyed, however, that on the day after the case ended, Cumming married an American heiress. Nevertheless, he ensured that Cumming was ostracized from Society, which meant virtual exile in the 1890s. Cumming spent much of his life after that at his large Scottish house, Gordonstoun, which later became the school to which the present Prince of Wales went.

William Gordon-Cumming, a baronet in the Scots Guards. After dinner on the first evening, a game of baccarat was started and two of the guests noticed that Cumming was apparently cheating by moving his bet forward or backwards when he thought no one was watching. He was confronted with this accusation and asked to sign a paper, which he reluctantly did, to say that he would never play cards again. The paper was signed by the other nine men who played cards that night, including the Prince of Wales. That was meant to be the end of this affair.

When the news got out, probably through Daisy Brooke, Gordon Cumming decided to bring an action against his accusers. In this civil action the Prince of Wales had to appear in Court, where he was cross-examined by Sir Edward Clarke for twenty minutes. He also had to sit in Court for six days. His conduct was further questioned because, as a Field Marshal, he should have known that when an officer's conduct was questioned the case had to be submitted to his Commanding Officer and this had he failed to insist upon.

THE RESTORATION, 1902

*E*dward succeeded to the throne at the age of 59. The Coronation was planned for 26 June 1902 – the crowds had gathered, the crowned heads had arrived, and the souvenir mugs had been printed with that date. But two days before the great event, it was announced that the King was seriously ill, and was to have an emergency operation. Some ten days earlier Edward had collapsed with a stomach pain and Queen Alexandra herself had to cut his belt with a knife. The royal doctors were reluctant to agree that an operation was necessary, since there was a real risk that he would die. Eventually they decided on an operation to remove his appendix, which saved his life. The public showed its fascination with royal illness – as it was to do with George V and George VI – and Punch's *Linley Sambourne* loyally welcomed his recovery.

The beneficiaries of the postponement were the charities for the poor in Whitechapel. They were given the huge mountains of food that had been prepared for the royal guests. The Coronation eventually took place on 2 August, but the crowned heads did not return, apart from the Abyssinians: they had never left, for they were worried they would lose face if they went home without seeing the great event.

The Lord Chief Justice summed up in favour of the defendant, although the popular press was on Gordon-Cumming's side. The verdict was greeted with hisses in the Court. Arriving at Ascot on the day after the verdict, the Prince of Wales was booed. The *New York Times* stated that 'Royalty is a burden to the British taxpayer for which he fails to receive any equivalent.' *The Times* wished that it was the Prince of Wales who had signed a declaration never to play cards again.

When Edward became King in 1901, he had become too set in his ways to change very much. But he did apply himself with vigour to fulfilling the royal role. He appreciated that people expected to see their King. Perhaps he had read Walter Bagehot's comment in his classic study of *The English Constitution*:

> Royalty is a government in which the attention of the nation is concentrated upon one person doing interesting actions . . . most people when they read that the Queen walked along the slopes of Windsor – that the Prince of Wales went to the Derby – have imagined that too much thought and prominence had been given to little things. But they had been in error; and it is nice to trace how the actions of a retired widow and an unemployed young man had become of such importance.

ILLUSTRATING THE FORCE OF
ANCIENT HABIT, 1903

This cartoon by Max Beerbohm appeared during Edward's visit to Paris in 1903. Edward's favourite high-class brothel in Paris was Le Chabonais, where the proud Madame showed to her other clients the chair in which he used to sit to pick the girl he wanted. In this cartoon, on a visit to a nunnery, he cannot break the old habit and says to the Mother Superior, 'Enfin, Madame, faîtes monter la première à gauche.' It is little wonder that, with cartoons like this, Max Beerbohm had to wait for his knighthood until after the Second World War.

L'ENTENTE CORDIALE, 1903

Edward spoke perfect French and always enjoyed visiting France, especially the theatres, restaurants and clubs in Paris. He spent every February in Biarritz and the Spring in the Mediterranean – being absent from Britain for about four months of the year. In 1903 he made an official visit to France and met President Loubet. There is no doubt that this visit encouraged an atmosphere of goodwill in France and reinforced the Government's foreign policy, aimed at improving relations.

Edward was keen to be in the limelight, either by making royal visits abroad or by welcoming visitors to Britain to help to enhance Britain's prestige. He had some influence in promoting the 1904 Entente Cordiale, the defensive alliance with France, and many French people believed that it was very much his personal style and enthusiasm that led to a greater friendship between the two countries. Edward was never much interested in the political struggles between the Parties and in politics he remained a very conventional figure.

EDWARD VII ENJOYS PARIS

In the year before he died Edward told his son that he had crossed the Channel six times that year. Throughout his life he was at home on the French Riviera and in Paris. In France, French detectives charted his way to his various amoreuses – the Princesse Sagan on a corner of the Esplanade des Invalides, or the Baronne Alphonse de Rothschild, or the Comtesse Edmond de Pourtailes, and any number of ladies at different hotels. When Edward stayed at L'Hôtel Bristol, he signed in as the Duke of Lancaster.

BABBLING ON THE THAMES, 1908

In 1908, the British public had become very concerned about the increase in German naval power. Parliament originally decided to build some battleships, but the cry arose: 'We want eight and we won't wait.' This

German cartoon, from Kladderadatsch, recognizes that Britain is re-equipping her Navy, though the words that appear at Belshazzar's feast refer to the new threat of aerial warfare, since Germany was already building the Zeppelin airships.

FIERCE IS THE LIGHT THAT BEATS AROUND THE CROWN, 1909

This unusual cartoon is an early example of the intrusive interest of the press in the monarchy. As the century wore on, the popular press found that anything the Royal Family did was of absorbing national interest. Their private lives had become public properties.

Sir Charles Dilke observed that Edward 'was a very strong Conservative and an even stronger jingo'. Yet he incurred his mother's fury in 1898 by acting as a pall-bearer at Gladstone's funeral. Victoria had always been jealous of the 'People's William'.

A life of indulgence began to take its toll. Edward could no longer stand up to shoot in his butt and he needed to be helped to go upstairs. He had punished his frame, his stomach and lungs over the years, and eventually they gave out.

It is interesting to see the way in which comment both in the press and in the cartoons changed when he became King. The tone became much more respectful. His great persecutor over the years, the radical *Reynolds News*, said at his accession, 'In any case the new king's wild days are over.' The conservative *Pall Mall Gazette* declared: 'In some truth, there is no more popular figure in the world today than His Majesty King Edward VII.' The English cartoons avoided any criticism, and the King is portrayed as a rather benign father-figure; there are none showing him with his mistresses. The French and some

German cartoons were more vigorously critical, but even that criticism died away after the end of the Boer War in May 1902.

During his reign, Edward became more popular, since the British public have a soft spot for a 'card', and they felt his heart was in the right place. He acquired the sobriquet, 'Edward the Peacemaker' and one popular music-hall song put it:

While we've got a King like good King Edward,
There ain't going to be no war!

THE PEACEMAKER, 1910

Edward VII did not welcome the fact that in his declining years he was involved in a constitutional crisis which might have led to him using his royal prerogative to create as many Liberal peers as the Prime Minister required. As an hereditary monarch,

Edward respected the rights of the House of Lords, but he knew that he would have to accept the advice of his Prime Minister, Asquith, here seen on the left, particularly after it had been reinforced by a General Election. Edward died before this crisis was resolved.

8 · George V

1910–1936

'Enough of your self-pitying!
The King is duller than the Queen.'

Max Beerbohm

GEORGE V, who was born in 1865, was the second son of the Prince of Wales and was not expected to succeed to the throne. His elder brother, Prince Eddy, was a simpleton. Even the crusty old Duke of Cambridge said of him, 'He was an incurable and inveterate dawdler, never ready, never there.' Eddy had earned the nickname of 'Collar and Cufs' because of his inordinate fascination with clothes and the fact that he wore very high collars, largely to conceal his long neck. In 1890, it had been rumoured that he had been involved in the Cleveland Street homosexual scandal; he was packed off for a long tour of India, to ensure that he was out of reach when the trials were taking place. Whether Prince Eddy had been involved or not, he was certainly being treated for venereal disease in 1890. When, in 1891, he suddenly contracted pneumonia and died, there was a general sense of relief.

Just before Eddy's death, he had become engaged to the Danish Princess May of Teck – an engagement that had been engineered by Queen Victoria and his parents. They had chosen a Princess whom they believed would make a good Queen of England, and they saw no reason to change their view. After a decent interval of twelve months, Mary was re-engaged to his brother, George. It turned out to be a very happy marriage, for they were well suited to each other. Edward Albert, later to be Edward VIII, was born in 1894 and their second son, Albert Frederick George (Bertie), later to be George VI, in 1895.

THE KING-EMPEROR, 1911

After his coronation in Westminster Abbey, George V travelled to India, with Queen Mary, in order to be installed as King-Emperor. In the whole period from 1876, when Victoria had become the Empress of India, until 1947, when India became independent,

George V was the only reigning monarch to visit his vast Empire in the Indian subcontinent. He liked India and particularly enjoyed the hunting and shooting of its wildlife. The Durbar in Delhi in 1911 was the grandest display of the splendour of the British Empire.

ARE WE AS WELCOME AS EVER?,
1911

Edward VII's circle of friends needed to be very rich in order to entertain him in the manner he expected. Some English families even bankrupted themselves in trying to do so. This is one of the reasons why Edward had a penchant for self-made men and he was particularly attached to Jewish financiers. In this cartoon by

Beerbohm, drawn shortly after Edward's death, two Rothschilds, Lord Burnham (Edward Lawson), Arthur Sassoon and Ernest Cassel are wondering whether they would still be welcome at the Court of the new King. They were not.

There was a strong streak of anti-semitism, which Edward disregarded, at the turn of the century. Ernest Cassel became his investment adviser and was rewarded with a knighthood and membership of the Privy Council.

George had a long period of training as Prince of Wales and during that time he was considerably helped by his father. For a change in the House of Hanover, father and son got on fairly well with each other. Edward allowed the Prince to see official papers, something which had been denied to him by his mother, Queen Victoria.

George ascended the throne at the age of 45 and during his reign of twenty-five years he had to deal with three constitutional and political crises that helped further to define the limits of a constitutional monarchy. The first occurred in 1910–11, soon after he had ascended the

This cartoon appeared in the Westminster Gazette *just after it was publicly announced that George V was prepared, if necessary, to create enough Liberal peers to swamp the Conservative majority in the House of Lords. The ancient nobleman is appalled at the prospect of hundreds of new peers – 'Mushrooms!'; and what's more, 'By George!'*

throne. Asquith's Liberal Government had just held a General Election, the purpose of which was to assert the right of the House of Commons to pass a Finance Bill, despite the disapproval of the House of Lords. The Liberal Government had been frustrated by the House of Lords over several measures, and Asquith was determined not only to remove the power of the House of Lords to reject a Finance Bill, but also to limit the delaying power of the Lords on any other Bill to two years. Asquith knew that another General Election would be necessary to confirm such a significant constitutional change. He also knew that if the House of Lords continued to resist these changes, he would have to ask the King to create enough peers to form a Liberal majority in the House of Lords and thus ensure that Bills were passed.

Asquith, after getting Cabinet approval, formally asked the King 'to exercise his constitutional powers, which may include the prerogative for creating peers'. In November 1910 he secured a secret understanding that the King would do this, but the pledge, surprisingly, did not leak out until the summer of 1911.

Although one of his Private Secretaries strongly objected to the King giving such a promise, George V accepted that he had to do so. He was very uneasy about making the decision, but realized that as a constitutional monarch he had to take the advice of his Prime Minister, however distasteful and unpleasant.

The second crisis was in 1923 following the resignation of the terminally ill Bonar Law as Prime Minister. As Bonar Law did not recommend a successor, George V had to use his prerogative to select one. The choice was between the experienced Lord Curzon, the establishment candidate, who clearly expected to be called, and Stanley

Many of the settlers in the British Empire were of relatively recent British origin. They looked upon Britain as home and the King, in London, as their King. In this Australian cartoon, from the Melbourne Punch, George V is being carried forward by the lion of Britain, the tiger of India, the moose of Canada, the kangaroo of Australia and the antelope of Africa. He says, 'Thank heaven, they're all good goers. There's not a jib among them.'

George V always took his position as head of the British Empire seriously. Although he rarely left England after 1918, he insisted that his son, the Prince of Wales, should regularly visit all parts of the Empire.

Baldwin, the rising Conservative politician who had only held ministerial office for quite a short time. The King chose Baldwin. Several considerations influenced his choice, not least his memory of how Curzon had treated him on a visit to India, but also the view that it was not feasible to have a Prime Minister in the House of Lords. It was a very sensible decision.

The third crisis was in 1931 when Ramsay MacDonald's Labour Cabinet was deeply divided about a programme of expenditure cuts necessary to deal with the financial crisis. George V, sensing trouble, returned from Balmoral, and MacDonald indicated that he might have to resign. With the Prime Minister's support, the King then saw Baldwin, the leader of the Conservatives, and Sir Herbert Samuel, who was standing in as leader of the Liberal Party since Lloyd George was ill. They both said they would serve in a National Government under MacDonald. The King then stage-managed meetings with all three; he was clearly in favour of a National Government, since it was preferable to a General Election at a time when the pound was under pressure.

George V flattered MacDonald and appealed to his national pride. Wigram, the King's Private Secretary, wrote of this event: 'Our captain played one of his best innings, with a very straight bat. He stopped the

SAILOR KING, 1914

*A*t the age of 12, George had been
sent off as a navy cadet, largely as
a companion to his simple elder
brother. Together they sailed round the
world for three years. He was the only
monarch to have his arms tattooed.
After thirteen years, he was capable
enough to be given command of a
torpedo boat, then a gunboat, and
finally a cruiser. In 1891, when George
was married, he wore the uniform of a
sea captain. Nevertheless, he was glad
to give up the sea, since he suffered
from sea-sickness and did not like
leaving England.

Beerbohm could not resist the irony
of George, at the beginning of the First
World War, being a 'Sailor King'. Many
soldiers resented the fact that the Navy,
in spite of one great engagement,
played a relatively minor role in the
War. But the War left an enduring
impression upon George, as it did on
everyone who lived through it, and,
towards the end of his life, he used to
refer to it as 'that horrible and
unnecessary war'.

rot and saved his side.' It was not quite clear what his 'side' was. The
Labour Party, which MacDonald headed, came out of it very badly:
only a handful of ministers joined the National Government and, in the
General Election later that year, it suffered utter disaster.

The King's role in this crisis can be exaggerated; it was clear that
he followed the advice of his Prime Minister, Ramsay MacDonald,
though that advice also happened to coincide with his own views.

THE KING AT THE FRONT, 1914

*I*n the First World War, the Prime Ministers, Asquith, then Lloyd George, were not the symbol of national unity: it was the King who came to represent the country. That was not the case in the Second World War, when Churchill fulfilled the role.

KING 'OFENHOCKER', 1914

*T*he German magazine, Jugend, saw George V in a different light – a shrunken shadow, compared to the massive lioness, Queen Victoria. As King 'Stay-at-home', he draws what comfort he can by saying, 'Colossal! I am the leader of Kitchener's army of 2 million.'

The Germans assumed that George V was as important as the Kaiser. He was not. In the disputes between Lloyd George and the Generals, the King sided with Haig but he had little influence on any of the major decisions, which were made by Lloyd George.

KING GEORG AN DER FRONT, 1915

*J*ugend *portrays an incident that occurred when George V was visiting his troops. On 28 October 1915, the King was provided by General Haig with a chestnut mare, which had been trained to withstand the sound of gunfire. When the horse heard twenty airforcemen cheering, however, it reared up and threw off the King. The horse rolled on to him and, if it had not been on soft ground, the King would probably have been killed. His injuries were not at first detected but, in fact, he had suffered a fractured pelvis and three cracked ribs. The injury left him permanently stiff.*

This German cartoon embellishes the incident. The other victim of the horse's activity is Raymond Poincaré, President of France.

King Georg an der Front

"Soldaten Englands und Frankreichs, empfangt meinen Dank und Gruß! Ich zweifle nicht, daß wir diesen gigantischen Kampf der Zivilisation gegen die Barbarei zu einem siegreichen Ende führen werden — — — —

Hopla!" — —

Throughout his reign, George V was conscious of the need to protect the institution of the monarchy. He believed that it would only survive if he set a high moral standard and abided by it. During the First World War, George was also concerned that the anti-German sentiment could wash over the throne. H.G. Wells, in 1917, had declared Buckingham Palace to be 'an alien and uninspiring court'. The anti-German sentiment had forced the resignation of the Lord Chancellor, Haldane, who had been educated in Germany, and the First Sea Lord, Prince Louis of Battenburg. In 1917 George thought it prudent to abandon the historic family name of Guelph and declared he wanted his dynasty to be known as 'The House of Windsor', a title suggested to him by his Private Secretary, Lord Stamfordham. When the Kaiser heard of the change, he said he was looking forward to attending the opera, 'The Merry Wives of Saxe-Coburg-Gotha'.

The King also acted to protect the crown in 1917 over the question of whether Tsar Nicholas II and his family should be given asylum in Britain. Lloyd George and the Cabinet were quite prepared to accept

George V 145

DIE UNHEILIGEN DREI KÖNIGE, 1916

'The Unholy Three Kings' appeared in the German magazine, Simplicissimus, published in Munich at the time of Epiphany in 1916, an important occasion in Catholic Bavaria. The 'Three Kings' are the Tsar Nicholas II, George V, and Raymond Poincaré, President of France. In 1916 America was still neutral, but one of its largest companies, the Bethlehem Steel Corporation, a major armaments manufacturer, supplied the allies. The star, which the Three Kings had been following, led them to the arms suppliers; myrrh and frankincense are absent from their gifts.

this, but George V was strongly opposed, on the grounds that he did not know what the family would do; they would be expensive to maintain; and supporting an unpopular monarch would not be good for the British throne. If, in 1917, a British ship had been sent to the Baltic, it was probable that the Russian regime at that time would have been glad to dispose of the Tsar and his family by sending them to exile in England. But George V did not throw out this lifeline to his cousin and he must carry some responsibility for the fact that a year later the entire Russian royal family was murdered.

George V was essentially an English country gentleman. He was happiest being the squire of Sandringham, where he could indulge his great passion for shooting. The only book that he would ever pick up, open and read with any sense of enjoyment was a game book. In his life, a good day would be to spend the morning shooting, the afternoon looking through his stamp collection, and the evening dining quietly with his family in the small house where they all lived on the Sandringham estate. Like his father, George V was a stickler for sartorial etiquette and, even when he dined at home with the family, he wore a white tie and the Garter Star. He continued to wear frock coats long after they had gone out of fashion.

George's whole lifestyle was wholesome but dull. He hated travelling abroad and, from 1918 to his death 18 years later, he spent only 8 weeks out of the country. Five of these were spent convalescing from a serious illness in the South of France. (As the train took him through France, it was alleged that he said, 'Pull down the blinds, Mary, abroad's bloody' – words that were to be echoed by Uncle Matthew in Nancy Mitford's *The Pursuit of Love*.)

The King also believed in the virtue of reticence. He deplored frank memoirs, like Margot Asquith's, and he once said jokingly to Baldwin that he was tempted to relate the interesting and extraordinary things that ministers had said to him. Baldwin apprehensively said, 'I hope, Sir, that you will not write autobiographical articles in the press.' George replied, 'Not till I am broke.' When he learnt that Lloyd George was going to publish his own account of the First World War, he expressed the hope that his former Prime Minister would not. Lloyd George, who had scant regard for George V, observed, 'He can go to hell. I owe him nothing, he owes his throne to me.'

Throughout his reign, the cartoons of George V were respectful. German magazines were an exception, but that is not surprising since the Kaiser was portrayed in *Punch* as a cruel and wicked aggressor. The leading cartoonist of the time was David Low and, though thousands

DIE SORGE DES LANDESVATERS, 1917

This seems to be the only cartoon in which George is depicted indulging in his favourite hobby of collecting stamps: he used to spend three afternoons a week browsing through his collection. As the war raged on the Western Front, the German cartoon by Blir emphasizes the triviality of the King's pastime: 'The Agony of the Father of the Nation'.

The King is also asking Lloyd George, 'Have you enough malt in reserve for my whisky?' This implies that George V, who had given a pledge not to consume any alcohol during the War as an example to his subjects, was in fact a secret drinker. That was certainly not true, because George V could always be depended upon to keep his word.

of his cartoons have been examined, one portraying George V is yet to emerge. Max Beerbohm drew just six cartoons of George V and they are full of delicious irony and witty malice. They were not published in the popular press, however, and were only seen by a small coterie of people in the West End of London who were interested in fine art.

It is sometimes said that George V invented the modern monarchy. That is an exaggeration. The role of the crown had been slowly changing for over 150 years. George appreciated that, while the monarchy had lost most of its constitutional powers, it none the less had a more formal and symbolic significance. He felt strongly that he had to set an example to others and the most effective way of doing that was to fashion an 'ideal royal family'. He also succeeded in a time of great political turbulence in creating a sense of serene continuity. His dullness fitted well with his decency and dignity. He was respected, much loved and left the crown in a strong position. Or, as Jimmy Thomas, the Labour Cabinet Minister, said of him: 'By God, he's a great 'uman creature.'

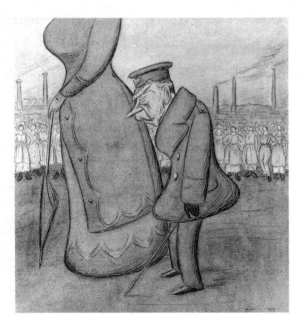

CHEERING UP THE MUNITION WORKERS, 1917

Queen Mary seemed to dwarf George V, as Beerbohm suggests. In fact, they were the same height, but the Queen's way of wearing her hair and her rather old-fashioned toque hats made her appear much taller. Chips Channon wrote in his diary, 'Her appearance was formidable, her manner – well, it was like talking to St Paul's Cathedral.' The novelist, E. M. Forster, was rather shortsighted; at Lord Harewood's wedding reception, he bowed to the cake thinking it was Queen Mary.

In 1917, one of George V's secretaries had to wrestle with the grave and serious question as to whether women munition workers, in a factory to be visited by the Queen, should or should not remove their gloves to shake hands.

THE SILVER JUBILEE, 1935

This is the tribute by Strube's Little Man to George V on his Silver Jubilee on 6 May 1935. George V had become a much-loved king. He had symbolized the country through the turbulence of the First World War and the Depression. His quiet dignity created a sense of stability and continuity which were both essential to the monarchy.

THE DEATH OF KING GEORGE V

Spirits of well-shot woodcock, partridge, snipe
Flutter and bear him up the Norfolk sky:
In that red house in a red mahogany book-case
The stamp collection waits with mounts long dry.

The big blue eyes are shut which saw wrong clothing
And favourite fields and coverts from a horse;
Old men in country houses hear clocks ticking
Over thick carpets with a deadened force;

Old men who never cheated, never doubted,
Communicated monthly, sit and stare
At the new suburb stretched beyond the run-way
Where a young man lands hatless from the air.

John Betjeman

9 · Edward VIII

January 1936 – December 1936

'Hark the Herald Angels Sing
Mrs Simpson's pinched our King'

Walter Savage Landor

EDWARD was forty-one years old when he succeeded to the throne. He was, by then, one of the most recognized and well-known people in the world. He was very popular in the United Kingdom, for the insecurity which troubled him all his life was not known and had not by then been revealed to the general public.

In the First World War, Edward was anxious to see active service, but Lord Kitchener, the first serving officer to be appointed War Minister, firmly refused, telling him that he might be killed, or even worse, taken prisoner and used as a hostage. He was consigned, much to his chagrin, to fairly trivial duties behind the lines. Even after the War he had to struggle to find things to do. With the encouragement of George V, he made official visits to many countries to enhance Britain's prestige and to promote her trade: the United States in 1919 and 1924; India in 1922; Canada, frequently, since he owned a ranch there; Australia; South Africa; and South America. As the bachelor heir to the British throne, he was the focus of attention and he undoubtedly had star quality.

Much of Edward's life was spent, inevitably, merely passing time in riding, dancing, golf and tennis. Unlike his father, he loathed shooting. He was frequently bored because he liked to be busy and active, and it is ironic that one of the most energetic Kings of England was destined to spend the latter part of his life in undemanding and footling activities. Edward said to his Private Secretary, Godfrey Thomas, in 1927: 'It is just the chronic state of being the Prince of Wales – of which I am so heartedly and genuinely fed up. It is just so nerve-wracking and distracting. Sometimes, Godfrey, I think I could go mad.'

George V did not like his son's lifestyle, his friends or the way he dressed. There was a steady flow of pernickety comments about Edward's clothes, and the Prince of Wales dreaded the tedium of visits to Sandringham and Balmoral. He found enjoyment and diversion in flirting. He had lost his virginity, following an arrangement made by

CLARK GABLE MEETS THE PRINCE OF WALES, 1924

This cartoon by the Mexican, Miguel Covarrubias, captures the shy, almost apologetic, manner of the Prince of Wales when meeting one of the great personalities of Hollywood. He is wearing a suit made from a cloth for which Edward became famous – the Prince of Wales check.

THE PRINCE OF WALES IN NEW YORK, 1924

When the Prince of Wales first visited America in 1919 he was fêted, but his visit in 1924 was rather less successful. The richest families in America had looked upon Edward as a 'good catch' for one of their daughters. One columnist said of this visit that, 'The bank balances of the refulgent chieftains of the Long Island set were pitted against His Royal Highness's health.'

Edward did manage to have some 'shore leave', and one English businessman complained that, on two occasions, he was so drunk he had to be taken home. His reputation was not helped by the fact that his boon companion, Fruity Metcalfe, left his wallet in the rooms of a New York prostitute, and it contained some letters from the Prince. There was generally a bad press, but it improved enormously after Edward gave a tea party to the seven leading editors: he knew how to handle the press.

fellow officers, with a prostitute in France during the War. He failed to find any young, unmarried and attractive British girls with whom to fall in love, or even to have an affair.

Edward's first great love, during the War, was almost certainly platonic. Lady Coke was the wife of the Earl of Leicester and twelve years

BRITAIN'S STAR COMMERCIAL TRAVELER PREPARES TO TAKE THE ROAD, 1930

In this cartoon by McCutcheon, which appeared in the Chicago Tribune, *Ramsay MacDonald, the Prime Minister, battling with the problems of the recession, turns to the Prince of Wales for help. Although Edward at times complained about the arduous duties of a royal tour, he travelled further and longer than any other monarch. From 1918 to 1925, Edward's stamina enabled him to visit forty-five countries, travelling 150,000 miles – none by aeroplane. People warmed to his diffident and unpompous style. In South Africa he was adored for speaking a few sentences in Afrikaans. For his visit to South America, he learnt Spanish quite quickly. He wrote to Queen Mary from Buenos Aires, 'I am picking up a little Spanish and tango as well, and neither are very difficult.'*

older than the Prince. She provided the role that Edward wanted most from a woman – a confidante and a comforter. In all his relationships with women, he craved to be mothered. In 1918 he met Freida Dudley Ward, when they were both sheltering after an air-raid warning. Their relationship lasted for fifteen years. She was married to a Liberal MP who was sixteen years older than herself; it was largely a marriage of convenience, but she had two daughters to whom Edward became an 'Uncle'. Edward was besotted with her and wrote virtually every day, and sometimes twice a day, in the early 1920s. Freida gave to him the reassurance that he needed. Their relationship was a huge folly, for the future King could not have any long-term relationship with a married woman: Edward was turning his back on reality; and it was an escape from responsibility.

After Freida, Edward had a fling with Thelma, Lady Furness, who introduced him to Wallis Simpson in 1931. Wallis had been married twice: first in 1916 to an American naval officer, who became an

CAN HE MAKE ONE WITHOUT
LOSING THE OTHER?, 1936

*This cartoon by Sweigert, from the
San Francisco Chronicle, sums up
the central dilemma of the Abdication
Crisis: could Edward really keep the
crown, marry Mrs Simpson and make
her Queen? The marriage was a very
high fence.*

alcoholic, after which they divorced in 1927; and secondly to Ernest
Simpson, the head of a firm of American shipbrokers. Simpson became
a naturalized British subject and served in the Coldstream Guards.

Over the years, Mrs Simpson has not had many friends and so it is
only fair to recognize that at the time of Edward meeting her, she had
a considerable allure. Cecil Beaton generously wrote: 'Her skin was
incredibly bright and smooth, like the inside of a shell, her hair as sleek
as only the Chinese women know how to make it. I liked her surprised
eyebrows when she laughs, and her face has great gaiety.'

Wallis Simpson was, however, a selfish person who wanted to dom-
inate all the men in her life, and Edward was easy meat. She undoubtedly aroused him sexually and there was some question as to whether
most women could. He returned that attraction with a slavish devotion. While Thelma Furness was in the United States in 1934, Wallis
and Edward became lovers, and she became virtually a resident at his
house, Fort Belvedere, in the grounds of Windsor Castle. Duff Cooper,
Tory Minister and close friend of Edward, claimed: 'She is as hard as
nails, and she doesn't love him.' Wallis treated Edward like a child,
often upbraiding him in public, which he would accept from no one
else. He replied by showering her with money and jewels.

KING'S VISIT TO SOUTH WALES, NOVEMBER 1936

*J*ust as the crisis was about to burst, Edward made an official visit to the depressed areas in South Wales, celebrated here by Strube. He uttered the famous words, 'Something must be done.' His sympathetic attitude to the unemployed endeared him to the country. Even the Socialist, H. G. Wells, could scarce forbear to cheer: 'He is unceremonious, he is unconventional, and asks the most disconcerting questions about social conditions.' Archbishop Temple wrote to thank Edward for 'the constant understanding and sympathy which Your Majesty has shown towards the working people of the country, especially the miners and the unemployed'.

UNEQUAL DISTRIBUTION OF WIVES, 1936

*T*his cartoon from the Chicago Tribune *shows that the American press was much more open than the British in dealing with the crisis. By early December the Cabinet, led by Baldwin, had decided that the King could not marry Mrs Simpson.*

THE CHOICE

THE PRIME MINISTER. "ALL THE PEOPLES OF YOUR EMPIRE, SIR, SYMPATHISE WITH YOU MOST DEEPLY; BUT THEY ALL KNOW—AS YOU YOURSELF MUST—THAT THE THRONE IS GREATER THAN THE MAN."

THE CHOICE, DECEMBER 1936

*B*ernard Partridge was the regular
Punch *cartoonist and he reverted to
the traditional role of the* Punch
*cartoon: speaking for the country.
Baldwin had got it right. Edward could
not have his cookie and the crown.*

*The relationship between Baldwin
and the King was very complex. At one
of their meetings, both burst into tears.
Baldwin wrote of Edward, 'He is an
abnormal being, being half-child, half-
genius. It is almost as if two or three
cells in his brain remain entirely
undeveloped, while the rest of him is a
mature man.'*

George V was deeply concerned about his son's frivolous lifestyle. He said, just before his death, 'He has not a single friend who is a gentleman . . . He does not see any decent society and he is forty-one.' Several times, the question of his marriage had arisen, and the whole range of European princesses had been carefully examined, but it was not until the 1930s that his father broached it with him and suggested that his bride could be an English woman without royal blood. By then it was far too late. George V prophetically said to Baldwin, 'After I am dead, the boy will ruin himself in twelve months.' This is exactly what Edward did, although it took him less than a year.

Edward became King in January 1936. He had decided by then that he could not live without Wallis Simpson and he intended to marry her as soon as she was divorced. After his succession, he talked of her as his future wife and, for the next seven months, he tried to manipulate events to ensure that his two ambitions, of wanting to marry Wallis and remain King, could be reconciled.

Discretion was thrown to the winds. In August 1936, Wallis accompanied him on a much-publicized yachting holiday around the Mediterranean, which the American press seized upon. In September, the Court Circular announced that she was staying at Balmoral, an event which even alarmed Winston Churchill – who had become the King's closest political supporter, though he was later to regret that. On 27 October, Mrs Simpson was divorced, but the Decree was conditional and not absolute, and a period of six months had to elapse to ensure that no evidence emerged to invalidate the divorce.

YOUNG EDWARD AND THE LION, 1936

The cartoonist Gabriel, drawing for the Daily Worker, *had no doubt who had won. At that time, Stanley Holloway's monologues were very popular and a real favourite was the one about young Albert, who stuck his stick in the lion's ear and was gobbled up. The amended verses run:*

Now young Edward had heard
  about lions,
how they were ferocious and wild
and to see Stanley lying so peaceful
didn't seem right to the child.

So straightaway the brave little
  fellow
not showing a morsel of fear
took his stick with the Royal arms
  on the 'andle
and poked it in Stanley's rear.

You can see that the lion didn't like
  it
and giving a kind of a roar
he pulled young Edward inside the
  cage with him
and swallowed the little chap whole.

SECRETLY IN THE DEAD OF NIGHT, 1936

*L*ow was reflecting the view of his employer, Lord Beaverbrook, that the establishment, led by Baldwin, had knocked the King off the throne against the wishes of the country. This was not correct. Over the weekend of 5 and 6 December, Baldwin had told his Tory MPs to go back to their constituencies and listen. When they returned on Monday, they reported the clear view of their constituents: that the King could not marry Mrs Simpson and remain on the throne.

The British press had been remarkably acquiescent. The divorce of Mrs Simpson, at an Ipswich court, had been barely reported, but the whole question was brought to a head by a speech from the Bishop of Bradford on the responsibilities of the King as the Head of the Church. The issue could no longer be evaded.

The strongest card held by the King was his popularity in the country. It was a card that Wallis Simpson repeatedly encouraged him to play and was reinforced by a famous visit to the South Wales coalfields in November 1936, where he expressed personal sympathy with the miners. The visit was so successful that Edward was encouraged to believe that he could get away with almost anything. By the beginning of December the King's future had become the central news in the country. The actual abdication crisis lasted only ten days.

The issue was startlingly simple: could a monarch, who was also the Head of the Church of England, marry a twice-divorced woman, although she had been the innocent party, and make her the Queen? As soon as more people became aware of what Mrs Simpson was like, she became very unpopular. She had to leave for the South of France; even there, she was hissed. Baldwin knew that the King could not get away with making her Queen: he knew that the British public would not stomach it. For a fleeting moment, the possibility of a morganatic marriage was considered, whereby Wallis Simpson would become the King's wife, but not the Queen. Baldwin and the Cabinet would not accept that and it was, in any case, of a dubious legal and constitutional validity.

After a weekend of crisis, Edward realized that there was insufficient support for him to marry Wallis Simpson and remain on the throne. On 11 December he abdicated – the first British King to do so. His radio broadcast to the nation, which he wrote himself in a very straightforward manner, including the words by which he will be remembered: 'You must believe me when I tell you that I have found it impossible to carry the heavy burden of responsibility, and to discharge my duty as King as I would wish to do, without the help and support of the woman I love.'

Edward was immediately created the Duke of Windsor and kept the title, 'His Royal Highness'. George VI was only too glad to support the view of his Cabinet that the same royal title should not be given to the Duchess of Windsor. This became a source of irritation, and Edward never forgave his brother and mother for not welcoming his wife. His niece, Queen Elizabeth II, did receive the Duchess of Windsor, but that did little to assuage the bitterness of the years of rejection.

During the Second World War, Edward became the Governor of the Bahamas, and afterwards the couple settled in a house near Paris, provided tax-free by the French Government. It was a long, dull and empty twilight, spent pottering about, looking more tanned and tired, as the years passed and their friends died away.

AT HOME WITH THE DUKE OF WINDSOR, 1960

*T*his drawing of Edward by Emmwood appeared in 1960 on the publication of his book, At Home with the Duke of Windsor. *After the War, when Edward and Wallis had settled in Paris, he augmented his investment income by writing. The first, in 1952, was his account of the Abdication,* The King's Story; *several others followed, including newspaper articles. The Duchess of Windsor's memoirs,* The Heart has its Reasons, *were particularly profitable. These journalistic earnings were needed to pay for their still-grand lifestyle and the generous entertaining that they kept up right to the end.*

10 · George VI

1936–1952

'For valour'

Churchill's inscription on George VI's funeral wreath

GEORGE VI did not expect to be King, and was dismayed when, in November 1936, his brother, Edward VIII, told him that he intended to marry Mrs Simpson. When it became clear, in early December, that George would have to succeed to the throne he recorded, 'I broke down and cried like a child.'

Born in 1895, George was always in the shade of his elder and more charismatic brother. As a child, he had to wear splints on his legs, though later he became a champion tennis player. At the age of eight he developed a stammer, but it was not until 1926 that he sought help to overcome this. Although his first name was Albert, and he was always known in the family as Bertie, on his accession he took his father's name and became George VI.

George's relationship with Edward became very distant. He soon cut off his elder brother's daily telephone calls of advice and, like Queen Mary, he refused to meet Mrs Simpson. George always had a suspicion that there would be a campaign to support the 'King over the Water', but there was never the faintest glimmer that that would happen in practice. The people felt betrayed by Edward VIII and were glad that they had a King who was happily married with two daughters – even though he was unknown, stammering, inexperienced, dull and rather dogged. The crisis of the monarchy was over.

From the diaries kept by George VI it was clear that he realized that he had few powers, but he certainly had political views. In 1940, when

LOVE, THE PILOT, 1923

*T*he best decision that George ever made was to marry Lady Elizabeth Bowes-Lyon, the youngest daughter of the Earl of Strathmore. She bolstered his confidence; sustained him through major crises, and created a truly happy home life. Without her, the history of the monarchy in the 20th Century might have been very different. After the Abdication, the country was relieved that it had a 'proper' King and Queen.

George was the first member of the Royal Family to become a fully qualified pilot.

SUNSHINE THROUGH DARK CLOUDS, 1936

*T*his is how the Montreal Daily Star
greeted the accession of George VI.
Britannia is saying, 'A new King reigns
on my throne with his good Queen to
help me carry on.' Neptune replies,
'. . . And the sunshine is breaking
through the dark clouds. "Carry on's'
the word, ma'am!"'

The Abdication could easily have
had a disruptive effect on the British
Empire, for almost the only formal link
between the self-governing dominions
and the United Kingdom was the
sovereign. If any of the dominions had
refused to accept the decision of the
Westminster Parliament in this matter,
it could have led to any one of them
becoming a republic, virtually
overnight. At one of his earliest
meetings with Edward VIII, Baldwin
had made great play of the fact that the
dominions would not accept Mrs
Simpson as Queen.

THE GOOD NEIGHBOURS, 1939

*G*eorge VI, unlike his father, decided
not to visit India for a Durbar. As
he said, 'I need time to settle in.' In
1939, however, he visited Canada and
the United States. President Roosevelt
welcomed George to his family estate
at Hyde Park and they clearly got on
very well together, for they stayed
talking until 1.30 am. They established
a good personal relationship,
represented here by Strube, which
served the two countries well during
the War. They were also brought
together by their love of smoking. Such

is political correctness today, however,
that the Trustees of the Roosevelt
Museum want to change their logo,
which is a jaunty silhouette of FDR
with his long cigarette holder.

THE ANSWER OF THE SEAS, 1940

This is one of the very rare cartoons of George VI during the War. The work of Illingworth in Punch, *it appeared while Neville Chamberlain was still Prime Minister. When Churchill became Prime Minister, in May 1940, he assumed the role of being the epitome of the nation – the cartoonists loved his cigars and his hats. In the thousands of cartoons in the Second World War Collection at the Imperial War Museum, there is not one that includes George VI. It was Churchill who became the symbol of national resistance.*

Neville Chamberlain had to resign, he recorded: 'I, of course, suggested Halifax.' Halifax was regarded as one of the arch-appeasers. He would have been a very unsuitable war leader. It was with reluctance that George accepted the inevitability of appointing Churchill, although later they became close friends. George VI also tried to intervene to stop Churchill appointing Beaverbrook as Minister of Production, but Churchill wisely ignored his letter.

At the end of the War, George's advice to Clement Attlee, who had become Prime Minister, was more fruitful. Attlee had told the King that he had it in mind to appoint Hugh Dalton as his Foreign Secretary and Ernest Bevin as the Chancellor of the Exchequer. George suggested that the talents of the two would be better suited if their roles were reversed. Attlee listened to this advice and then appointed Ernest Bevin as the Foreign Secretary; Bevin turned out to be one of the most successful men to hold that office.

The country came to respect George VI. His kingship was not the subject of any criticism or satirical attack. He had taken over as King with no enthusiasm; he did his duty; and he applied himself diligently to doing the job as well as he could. During the Blitz, the King and Queen and their children all stayed in London even though Buckingham Palace had been hit nine times. George was a thoroughly decent person.

IN THE ROYAL BEDCHAMBER, 1940

It is virtually impossible to find any cartoons that are in any way critical of George VI. This one appeared in a Spanish newspaper in 1940, at a time when the United States was offering fifty over-aged but serviceable destroyers to assist Britain, in exchange for allowing them to run bases in the West Indies and Newfoundland. To an anxious question from the Queen, the King is saying, 'There is a rumour that Churchill wishes to exchange me for a destroyer.'

This cartoon was reproduced by Reynolds News in 1944 to prove that Spain had been deeply hostile to British interests in the darkest days of the War, and that she should be punished for that. The newspaper was critical of Churchill's Government for acting too deferentially towards Franco.

It is difficult to underestimate the immense contribution that Queen Elizabeth made not only in bolstering the King's confidence but in making the monarchy popular again. During the Blitz, she said: 'The children won't ever leave without me; I won't leave without the King, and the King will never leave.' After Buckingham Palace had been bombed, she said: 'I am glad we have been bombed; I feel I can look the East End in the face.' She had the gift of making anyone she spoke to or smiled at, think they were the sole recipient of her warmth and interest. Wherever Queen Elizabeth went crowds cheered with real enthusiasm. Queen Mary had been respected as a royal figure, Queen Elizabeth was loved as a real person.

George died quite young, at the age of 57 years, from lung cancer, after he had spent his last day enjoying his favourite sport of shooting. During the War, he had created the George Cross and the George Medal for outstanding acts of bravery. Churchill, who had become Prime Minister for the second time a few months earlier, sent to his funeral a wreath of white lilacs and carnations in the shape of a George Cross with the simple words, 'For valour'.

UNDER THE SPLENDID EMPIRE TREE, 1945

When he was Duke of York, George had established an annual gathering of boys between the ages of 17 and 19, who were nominated in equal numbers by public schools and industrial firms. These were known as the Duke of York's Camps and one of the jollier moments occurred when all the campers sat around with the Duke of York and sang the old scouting song, Under the Spreading Chestnut Tree.

During the Second World War, the Empire rallied in support of the Mother Country. The role of the King as head of the Empire was crucially important.

11 · Elizabeth II

1952–

'Scrutiny . . . can be just as effective if it is made with a touch of gentleness, good humour and understanding'
Elizabeth II

As with many of her predecessors, it did not at first seem at all likely that the present Queen would ever inherit the throne – still less that she would do so quite early in life. At the time of her birth in 1926, her father's elder brother, Edward Prince of Wales, was in excellent health, and the most eligible bachelor in the world. There was every reason for expecting him to beget a line of heirs. Even if, by some chance, her own father, the Duke of York, eventually became King, Princess Elizabeth's right to the succession would be set aside in the possible event of her parents having a son. Yet Elizabeth was to have no brothers, her uncle's reign would end in circumstances without precedent, and her father was to die in his fifties.

The reign began with that rare occurrence in the history of the British monarchy: a respected and well-loved king was succeeded by a respected and well-loved heir. Queen Elizabeth was happily married, with a growing family; since she succeeded at the age of 26, a long reign stretched before her.

Britain's position in the world after the Second World War was one of transformation from a leading to medium-sized world power. This was a painful political adjustment, made no easier by successive governments failing to create a strong and expanding economy.

In the early part of the reign, most commentators continued to treat the Queen and the monarchy as they had done for most of the 20th Century. The favourite word journalists used to describe the Queen on her public appearances was 'radiant'. In those relatively few cartoons of the period where she figures at all, Elizabeth II appears as an icon, just as her father and grandfather had done. Many great changes were in fact taking place, which were profoundly to affect the popular view, but few, if any, of them are attributable to any changes in the personality or attitudes of the Queen herself.

The first change affected the Queen's position in the Commonwealth. During the first twenty years of Elizabeth's reign, virtually all

BIRTHDAY GREETINGS, 1947

E. H. Shepard drew cartoons for Punch, although he was more famous for his illustrations for the Winnie-the-Pooh books. Most of his cartoons were congratulatory, in the kind and respectful tradition of Punch.

Elizabeth said in a radio broadcast at the time: 'I declare before you all that my whole life, whether it be long or short, shall be devoted to your service, and the service of our great Imperial Commonwealth to which we all belong.'

STORK INVESTITURE, 1948

*P*rince Charles, the eldest of the Queen's four children, was born a little over a year after the marriage. This cartoon still retains the respectful, good-humoured approach.

MORNING AFTER, 1952

*D*avid Low criticized the public money that was spent on the Coronation celebrations. After the cartoon appeared, six-hundred readers wrote to complain about it.

of the former colonies in the British Empire became self-governing republics, most with their own heads of state, but recognizing the Queen as the head of the Commonwealth. Most of them remained in the Commonwealth and the Queen spent a good deal of time shoring up these new relationships. This was indeed a far cry from Winston Churchill's declaration that he had not become Prime Minister to preside over the liquidation of the British Empire.

The principal links of the new Commonwealth were based on nostalgia, trade, common political interest, sporting activities – and the personal efforts of the Queen. She looked forward to the biennial meetings of the heads of Government. Some of the new countries were direct offspring of the Mother Country; all of them had absorbed some part of the British way of doing things. The Queen's clear enjoyment and pride was not shared by all of her Prime Ministers, notably Margaret Thatcher, who did not relish being subjected to lectures from various heads of Commonwealth countries.

Secondly, the remaining constitutional powers of the monarchy were also disappearing. In 1957 and 1963 the Queen had to choose a Conservative Prime Minister when the incumbent resigned. On the first occasion the outgoing Prime Minister, Anthony Eden, did not recommend a successor; the Queen took soundings and made the decision she thought the Cabinet and the Conservative Party wanted. In 1963, she visited Harold Macmillan in hospital to receive his advice, which, by that time, had been massaged to ensure that the person he did not want, the favourite, R. A. Butler, was not summoned by the Queen. In the cartoons of these two events the Queen does not appear, for it was still an age of deference, and it was the politicians who took the brunt of the attacks.

THE DIGNITY OF THE THRONE, 1955

Princess Margaret, the younger sister of the Queen, fell in love with Group Captain Peter Townsend, who had been appointed an equerry to King George VI in 1944. Unfortunately, he was married, though in the process of obtaining a divorce. In 1953, Princess Margaret asked the Queen for permission to marry him, which was still necessary under George III's Royal Marriages Act of 1772. Princess Margaret was asked to wait for one year and decided in fact to wait a further year until she was twenty-five, the age at which she could marry whomsoever she wished. Townsend also told the Queen's Private Secretary, Alan Lascelles, whose reaction was: 'You must be either mad or bad.'

Lascelles alerted the Government and the Prime Minister, Winston Churchill, to the problem: the third-in-line to the throne, the sister of the Head of the Established Church, marrying a divorced man. In 1955, the Cabinet, now led by Anthony Eden, who himself had been divorced, decided that if Margaret were to marry Townsend, she would have to lose both her right to succeed to the throne and

But, mindful of the Church's teaching that Christian marriage is indissoluble, and conscious of my duty to the Commonwealth, I have resolved to put these considerations before any others.

her annual income from the civil list. In effect, she would be cast out of the Royal Family. After much soul-searching, she decided in October 1955 not to marry Townsend. Cartoon by Illingworth.

On both occasions the Queen acted according to the constitutional precedent established in the 20th Century. Her behaviour contrasted sharply with Queen Victoria's after Gladstone's retirement in 1894, when – without asking the departing Prime Minister for advice or making any effort to determine whom the Liberal Party might prefer – she chose the highly unsuitable Lord Rosebery as his successor.

However, even that remaining power of selecting a Prime Minister on the basis of advice provided was taken from Queen Elizabeth's hands. The Labour Party had already established a system of election for its Leader and that was used when Harold Wilson resigned as Prime Minister in 1976. The Conservative Party, in 1965, had also introduced a system of election for its Leader; it was used in that year, again in 1975 and once more in 1990. When Margaret Thatcher resigned in 1990, she remained Prime Minister until her successor was elected. The Queen, therefore, no longer has a role in the selection of a Prime Minister when there is a party with a clear majority, though she would still have a limited role in a hung Parliament.

'Maud dear, pray explain to me exactly what it is out of which dear Prince Philip is so eager that we should all take our finger.'

MAUD, DEAR, 1961

Prince Philip has been renowned for his bluntness. In 1961 he told British businessmen, 'Just at this moment of time, we are suffering a national defeat comparable to any lost military campaign, and what is more, self-inflicted. Gentlemen, I think it is about time we pulled our fingers out.' Here was a refreshing outburst of frankness, expressed in a way that no previous member of the Royal Family would have used in public. Osbert Lancaster did not draw many cartoons about the monarchy but, when he did, they were witty though benign.

Lancaster invented the pocket cartoon, which appeared on the front page of the Daily Express: *a newspaper that Prince Philip once described as 'A bloody awful newspaper. It's full of lies, scandal and imagination.' This was said before some of the tabloids, the* Sun *and the* Daily Mirror, *had got their claws into the Royal Family.*

SAINTS AND SINNERS, 1961

The most prolific cartoonist of the Royal Family was Giles, who was a life-long socialist and supporter of the trade unions. In his down-to-earth way, he reflects the rather old-fashioned attitude of the man-in-the-street towards the Royal Family – friendly and respectful – and his cartoons are good-humoured.

Like all royal consorts, Prince Philip had to fashion out his own role. As an athlete, he established the Duke of Edinburgh Award Scheme for young people and actively promoted the establishment of more playing fields across the country. For this, he was awarded sainthood by Giles. But, as he played polo on Sundays, he was technically a sinner. The Saints and Sinners was a club of sportsmen who raised money for charity.

When John Major was undergoing a bout of unpopularity in 1994 and early 1995, there was speculation that he might resign. The question arose as to whether the Queen would call a General Election if John Major so advised, even though there was a Conservative majority in the House of Commons. As John Major did not resign, we will not know the answer to this constitutional conundrum, but in all probability she would have accepted the advice of her Prime Minister. Throughout her reign, she has acted quite properly as a constitutional monarch, restricting involvement in politics to the minimum.

THE QUEEN OPENS PARLIAMENT, 1964

*P*rivate Eye *first appeared in 1961 and pioneered the satirical bubble caption. In the 1960s, the Prime Ministers were better and more frequent targets than the Royal Family. This is the comment on Harold Wilson's first Queen's speech and the scatological comment is constitutionally accurate.*

ON BEHALF OF THE FRENCH SPEAKING PEOPLES OF THE WORLD, 1967

*I*n 1964, the Government had expressed qualms about the Queen visiting Canada – a view not shared by the Canadian Government – but the Queen went ahead. By then, De Gaulle had made his famous balcony declaration, 'Vive Québec, Libre'. This Canadian cartoon by Duncan MacPherson was given to the Queen on her visit in 1967 and underlined the two national strands that make up Canada. The Queen, unlike her father and grandfather, was able to thank the Canadians in fluent French.*

I WAS ONLY JOKING, 1965

*T*his Franklin carton appeared in the Daily Mirror. It is interesting because, even as late as the 1960s, it was not customary to show the Queen's face in cartoons.

PRINCE OF WALES, 1969

Charles was crowned Prince of Wales in July 1969 at Caernarfon Castle, having spent the previous summer term at Aberystwyth University learning Welsh. The ceremony was planned by his uncle, Anthony Armstrong-Jones, as a television spectacular, and a new crown was designed for the event. This stimulated Ralph Steadman who, together with Scarfe, had revolutionized cartooning in the 1960s by bringing back violence and crudity to their drawings of politicians. The Royal Family, however, was exempt. Steadman remembers a cartoon he drew of the Queen, for a magazine called Man About Town, *being rejected by its owner, Michael Heseltine. In the 1970s, it was not only bad form to attack the Royal Family in cartoons, but it was also not good for the circulation of papers and magazines.*

The third influence which has had a significant effect on the Crown since Queen Elizabeth's accession is the mass media, which have taken an almost obsessive interest in every aspect of the Royal Family.

The Queen realized that the monarchy could not ignore the media by leading a private and discreet existence with only occasional forays into public events. The tone was set from the start. The Queen insisted, against the advice of the Archbishop of Canterbury and her Prime Minister, Winston Churchill, that her Coronation should be televised, and in particular that the most solemn events within the Abbey should be seen by all her subjects. It was an immense success. A further step was taken in 1969 when the BBC was allowed to make a film, 'The Royal Family', which showed the Queen, her husband and her children living as a family. The Crown was no longer a remote institution surrounded by mystery and protected by reverence. A further film, made in 1991, examined a year in the life of the Queen, and was also well received.

There was a conscious effort to make the monarchy more informal. In 1970 the 'royal walkabout' was invented to allow as many people as possible to meet the Queen and other members of the Royal Family. As a result of all these changes, the Royal Family, which George VI had referred to as 'The Royal Firm', became the most famous family in the world. But the press was no longer prepared to let it live in privacy, hidden behind the walls of Buckingham Palace, Windsor Castle, Balmoral and Sandringham.

In particular, its marital affairs became the stuff of popular journalism. The press, which turned a blind eye to the extra-marital adventures of Edward VII and of Edward VIII as Princes of Wales, has swooped on every salacious detail of the modern Royal Family with savage glee, and on more than one occasion has probably wrecked permanently the happiness of the individuals concerned. The press picked on one member of the family at a time. The first to get the full treatment was Princess Margaret. Her many suitors, her rejection of Group Captain Peter Townsend, her marriage to Anthony Armstrong-Jones, which was dissolved in 1979, were all exposed to the public gaze. Even after that, the unhappy woman was given little peace.

The media, however, were only limbering up for what was to follow. There was immense and natural interest in whom the Prince of Wales might marry. It was suggested that any future Queen had to be an aristocrat, a Protestant, attractive and a virgin. Few met all four requirements. When, in July 1981, Prince Charles married the beautiful Diana Spencer, it was the apogee of the greatest soap opera in the world. Within six months the Queen had to ask newspaper editors to respect the privacy of the pregnant Princess of Wales. Everything that the couple did and everything their friends said about them was front-page news. With that degree of publicity it was almost impossible for any relationship to survive.

PUNCH JUBILEE, 1977

*T*he twenty-fifth anniversary of the
Queen's reign saw a genuine
outburst of rejoicing. The street party, a
characteristic of the victory
celebrations in 1945, was revived and
Trog makes Elizabeth the Eastenders'
favourite, a Pearly Queen.

From 1990 the monarchy was submerged in a series of tidal waves, all involving the marriages of three of the Queen's children. Each one was driven onto the rocks and some of the media seemed only too glad to speed them on their way to disaster. All previous taboos were abandoned: the *Sun* published a picture of a naked Duke of York without his consent; private telephone calls made by the Prince and Princess of Wales were printed verbatim; and compromising photographs of the Duchess of York were published. The Crown and the Royal Family had not been subjected to such constant and scornful onslaught for over two hundred years.

"If HRH puts her horse down in that puddle once more, HRH is going to lose quite a lot of my goodwill."

PRINCESS ANNE, 1972

Princess Anne has been relatively well-treated by cartoonists. In 1971 she won the European Three-Day Event Championship and in 1976 was chosen for the British Olympic Horse Team. She said, 'When I appear in public, people expect me to neigh, grind my teeth, paw the ground and swish my tail.' Giles shows both her love of riding and her irritation with the intrusive press, at whom occasionally she swore. Her marriage to Captain Mark Phillips, its subsequent breakdown and her re-marriage did not evoke many cartoons. Cartoonists reflect the judgment of the country, that Princess Anne is 'a good thing'.

THE ROYAL FAMILY, 1970

*A*n unconventional portrait group
by Steadman.

MY HUSBAND AND I, 1972

*O*n her accession the Queen was
granted a Civil List of £452,000
each year to meet the official costs of
the monarchy. It was intended to
remain at that level for her reign, but
by 1972 inflation had eroded it
significantly. After a Parliamentary
review, a new level was agreed,
accompanied by further periodic
reviews. For the decade from 1990 the
Civil List is set at £7.9m a year, though
the Exchequer receives from the Crown
lands – which George III surrendered
in 1760 – some £80m a year. Not a bad
deal for the State. Few have grudged
the Queen the running costs of the
monarchy, but the list of the annuitants
supported by the Civil List and her
personal wealth have been sources of
irritation. Recognizing this, the Queen
agreed in February 1993 to pay income
tax on her personal income. Cartoon
by McLachlan.

ROYAL VISIT TO SAUDI ARABIA, 1979 *A role reversal, drawn by Steadman.*

The difficulty was compounded by various newspapers taking sides, no doubt with some encouragement from the main players and their friends. It was all reminiscent of the clash between George IV and Caroline of Brunswick, with the difference that both George and Caroline richly deserved the treatment they received, whereas Charles and Diana did not.

A sensational biography, *Diana, Her True Story*, was written by a committed republican, and serialized in *The Sunday Times*, in 1992 – so the quality press pitched in as well. At the end of 1992, John Major announced to the House of Commons that the Prince and Princess of Wales had decided to separate; the Queen made a celebrated speech in which she referred to 'the *Annus Horribilis*'. She said, as explicitly as she could, that the press should be less venomous: 'Criticism is good for people and institutions that are part of public life. No institution should expect to be free from the scrutiny of those who give it their loyalty and support, not to mention those who don't. But we are all part of the same fabric of our national society and that scrutiny by one part of another can be just as effective if it is made with a touch of gentleness, good humour and understanding.' Her plea was in vain.

THE QUEEN MOTHER

Not even Scarfe could find anything nasty in the Queen Mother, who has become the most beloved figure of the Royal Family. In 1937, her serene manner and the confidence she gave her husband did much to uphold the status of the crown after the Abdication. Similarly, in the 1990s, when her grandchildren were facing all manner of matrimonial troubles, she became once again the embodiment of all that was best in the Royal Family.

Elizabeth II 179

AT LEAST THERE'S NO DANGER . . ., 1979

*W*hen Margaret Thatcher became
Prime Minister in May 1979,
people wondered how the Queen
would deal with a woman Prime
Minister and vice versa. The Queen
took it in her stride. Margaret Thatcher
has a deep respect for the monarchy
and no one curtsied before the Queen
lower than she did. Cartoon by Giles.

FATHER AND SON, 1981

*T*his cartoon by Steve Bell
prophetically contrasts the macho
Prince Philip with the gentler Prince
Charles having his backbone stiffened
up by his new wife. Father and son
played polo until the Prince was
persuaded to give up such a dangerous
sport.

OFFICES TO LET, 1992

*P*rince Charles has been forthright in
his dismissal of modern architecture
– 'carbuncles'. He prefers traditional
stone, bricks and tiles to concrete and
glass, and he is putting his ideas into
practice by building an ideal village on
one of his estates. Although he has
been attacked for daring to express his
own views, they are close to those of
many of his future subjects – good
popular stuff. Cartoon by Hellman.

THE PRESS, 1981

*A*s the Queen's children grew up, they all became the focus of intense interest from the press. The photographers became much more intrusive and their capacity to capture the secret, private and intimate moment was transformed by the developmnt of the telephoto lens. Cartoon by Jensen.

THE QUEEN'S ANSWER

*O*n one visit, the Queen started to snap the photographers. The Palace realized that the monarchy could not hide behind the doors of privacy; but making it more accessible to newspapers and magazines was feeding an appetite that could never be satisfied. Cartoon by Trog.

THE ROYAL WEDDING, 1981

*T*he wedding of Lady Diana Spencer and Prince Charles in 1981 was, in the words of the Archbishop of Canterbury, 'The stuff of which fairy-tales are made.' Their first son, William was born in 1982, and their second, Harry, in 1984.

MARRIAGE BREAK-UP, 1992

*A*fter a disastrous visit to India,
*where Princess Diana was
photographed alone in front of the Taj
Mahal, it was no longer possible to
maintain the pretence that this was a*
*happy marriage. In December 1992, the
Prime Minister, John Major,
announced to the House of Commons
that the Prince and Princess of Wales
had decided to separate: the dream was
over. Cartoon by Garland.*

FERGIE'S FINANCIAL ADVISER, 1992

*S*arah Ferguson married Prince
*Andrew, the Queen's second son, in
1988, and they became the Duke and
Duchess of York. They had two
daughters, but their marriage came to
an end in 1993. The Duchess of York
decided to make a career as a writer of
children's books. Her name was linked
with several men and she was
photographed in a compromising
position with a certain John Bryan,
whom the world learnt was her
financial adviser. From* Private Eye.

In previous times, the tabloid newspapers had been among the most loyal and respectful parts of the press, but they now found that royal scandals were very good for their circulation. Both the Prince and the Princess of Wales turned to the press to justify their own actions. In 1994, Prince Charles allowed Jonathan Dimbleby to make a long film for the BBC about his life, followed by publication of a book. This featured many positive aspects of the Prince's public activities, but it also brought out into the open that Camilla Parker Bowles had been Charles' mistress for a number of years. The Princess of Wales responded by having her case put forward in another book and in 1995 giving a celebrated interview to BBC Television's *Panorama*. In this she laid claim to be a roving ambassadress and the Queen of Hearts, while questioning her husband's suitability to succeed. All this was red meat for the cartoonists – lovers, mistresses, bedside romps and nudity all returned with a vengeance.

'Look on the bright side, old girl, there's only 21 days of Annus Horribilis left.'

ANNUS HORRIBILIS, 1992

In a speech at the end of the year, the Queen called the fortieth of her reign the 'Annus Horribilis'. The marriages of three of her children had broken up; a fourth remained unmarried; and a few days before her speech a large part of Windsor Castle had burned down. It was an astonishingly frank admission of the turmoil that was besetting the House of Windsor and all the more poignant since hitherto the Queen had been the mistress of understatement.

SECONDS OUT, 1994

*L*ike George IV and Queen Caroline, the Prince and Princess of Wales each used the press to advocate their own case. Princess Diana's was put in Diana, Her Own Story *and in her* famous Panorama *interview, Prince Charles's in a TV series and book by Jonathan Dimbleby. The series and the interview were watched by millions, who seemingly liked the enticing exposure of their personal affairs. Cartoon by Heath.*

ICH DIEN, 1994   *Peter Brookes's comment.*

IF HISTORY REPEATS ITSELF, 1994

In 1994, the Queen visited Russia, the first such visit since the murder in 1918 of her remote relations, Tsar Nicholas II and his family. Rowson, who draws for the Guardian *and* Time Out, *is an avowed republican who depicts the Royal Family with ridicule and contempt. Here, the Russian* soldiers *do not have to bother to shoot the Royal Family because they are destroying themselves.*

Yet not even in 1993 and 1994, which was the low period of Queen Elizabeth II's reign from the point of view of the status of the Crown, did republicanism acquire any significant following.

BUT YOU ONLY NEED A MINI-CROWN NOW, YOUR MAJESTY, 1995

Tony Blair is depicted as being softer on Europe than John Major. Cummings makes an eloquent comment upon the transfer of power from Britain to the various European institutions. The Queen here is symbolic because the real transfer of power is from the Prime Minister, the Cabinet, Parliament and the Courts of Britain.

"But you only need a mini-crown, now, Your Majesty!"

KING CHARLES III

This cartoon appeared in the Daily Star *after the television programme in which Prince Charles effectively* admitted having an affair over a number of years with Camilla Parker Bowles. This admission fuelled speculation about what the position would be after his accession.

How has the monarchy been affected? The Queen has remained above the fray, virtually immune from attacks. This is even more true of the Queen Mother, who has come to embody the normality that characterized the Royal Family in the reigns of George V and George VI. She carries with her the hope that it will one day return. The cartoons show her as a lovable grandmother who likes a drop of gin and a flutter on the horses, but the genuine love of most of the nation towards her is tinged with sympathy. The steadfastness of the Queen and the Queen Mother in the early 1990s was essential in upholding public respect for the monarchy.

The celebration of the fiftieth anniversary of VE Day in June 1995 and the 95th birthday of the Queen Mother in August saw the spontaneous outbreak of love and affection for the Queen and Queen Mother. They were fulfilling the traditional role of a constitutional hereditary monarchy: the epitome of the national memory; the reassurance of a continuing tradition; and the focus of national loyalty.

PRINCE WILLIAM, 1995

In August 1995, Lord Wakeham, Chairman of the Press Complaints Commission, warned newspapers to respect the privacy of the thirteen-year-old Prince William, once he had started school at Eton. 'Prince William must be allowed to run, walk, study and play at Eton free of the fear of prying cameras.' He had intended a shot across the bows of the tabloids. But when Prince William started in September, Wakeham's advice was not followed. This cartoon by Morris appeared in the Inverness Press and Journal *the following day.*

■ **"I didn't know you were interested in photography, Ponsonby Minor."**

Illustration Acknowledgments

Associated Newspapers : Emmwood 159; Illingworth 169. Kenneth Baker Collection 5; 12 (t.r.); 33; 38; 48; 49; 52; 53; 54 (t.); 54 (b.); 55; 56 (b.); 57 (t.); 58; 59; 61 (t.); 61 (b.); 63; 64; 67; 68 (t.); 68 (b.); 70; 71; 72; 73 (t.); 73 (b.); 74 (t.); 74 (b.); 75; 76 (t.); 76 (b.); 77 (l.); 77 (r.); 78 (b.); 79; 80; 84; 88 (t.); 88 (b.); 89; 92 (t.); 92 (b.); 93 (t.); 93 (b.); 97; 98; 99; 100 (t.); 101; 102; 103; 107 (r.); 108 (t.); 108 (b.); 109; 116 (r.); 117 (l.); 118 (l.); 123; 124; 126; 127 (b.); 127 (t.l. and r.). Max Beerbohm (courtesy Mrs Eva Reichmann) 117 (r.); 133; 140; 148; 152. Steve Bell 181 (t.). Trustees of the British Museum, London 12 (l.); 19; 20 (b.); 21 (b.); 22; 23 (t.); 24 (b.); 26; 27; 28; 29 (t.); 29 (b.); 30; 31; 35; 36; 37; 39; 40; 41; 42; 43; 46 (t.); 46 (b.); 47; 51; 57 (b.); 105; 106 (t.). Peter Brookes 186 (b.). Bill Caldwell : *Daily Star* 188. Cartoon Study Centre, University of Kent 155 (t.); 158; 159; 170; 175. *Chicago Tribune* : McCutcheon 153; 155 (b.). Michael Cummings 2. Express Newspapers plc : Cummings 187 (b.); Giles 171; 176; 180; Osbert Lancaster 170; Strube 155 (t.); 162 (b.). Franklin 172 (b.). Gabriel 157. Garland 17, 184 (t.). Griffin 16; *Daily Mirror* 185. Hellman 181 (b.). House of Lords Library 56 (t.); 66; 69; 95; 96. Imperial War Museum 146. *The Independent* : Heath 186 (t.). *Inverness Press and Journal* : Morris 189. Kal 15. Leyden 168 (t.). Ewan MacNaughton Associates, c *The Telegraph* plc, London 1996: Jensen 182 (t.). Duncan MacPherson 172 (m.). McLachlan 177 (b.). *Montreal Daily Star* 162 (t.). National Portrait Gallery, Scotland 87. *The New Yorker* : Covarrubias 151. Piccadilly Gallery, London 143. *Private Eye* 172 (t.); 184 (b.). *Punch* : 161; Illingworth 8, 163; Partridge 156; E.H. Shepard 165, 167. *Reynolds News* 164. Martin Rowson : *The Guardian* 187 (t.). *San Francisco Chronicle* : Sweigert 154. Gerald Scarfe 179. Michael Shea Collection 15, 136, 182 (b.). Solo Syndication & Literary Agency : Low 158; 168 (b.). Ralph Steadman 173; 177 (.); 178. Trog 175, 182 (b.). Courtesy of the Board of Trustees of the V&A 1. John Ward-Roper Collection 45; 65.

Key t. = top; t.l. = top left; t.r. = top right; m. = middle; b. = bottom; l. = left; r. = right

Text Acknowledgments

Lines from 'The Death of King George V' (p. 149) by John Betjeman are reproduced from *Collected Poems* by kind permission of John Murray (Publishers) Ltd.

Index

Numerals in *italics* indicate illustration captions.